GRITTY CITIES

A SECOND LOOK AT

ALLENTOWN   BETHLEHEM   BRIDGEPORT

HOBOKEN   LANCASTER   NORWICH

PATERSON   READING   TRENTON

TROY   WATERBURY   WILMINGTON

GRITTY
CITIES

Mary Procter and Bill Matuszeski

 Temple University Press
Philadelphia

HT
123
.P76

Library of Congress Cataloging in Publication Data

Procter, Mary, 1942–
  Gritty cities.

  Bibliography: p.
  1. Cities and towns—United States—Case studies.
I. Matuszeski, William, 1941–   joint author.
II. Title.
HT123.P76   301.36′3′0973   78-15149
ISBN 0-87722-143-X
ISBN 0-87722-144-8 pbk.

Temple University Press, Philadelphia 19122
© 1978 by Temple University. All rights reserved
Published 1978
Printed in the United States of America

CONTENTS

PREFACE   vii

INTRODUCING THE GRITTY CITIES   3
The Gritty Cities in the Industrial Revolution   7
The Mills   13
The Neighborhoods   17
Downtown   23

ALLENTOWN   33
BETHLEHEM   51
BRIDGEPORT   71
HOBOKEN   91
LANCASTER   111
NORWICH   129
PATERSON   151
READING   169
TRENTON   187
TROY   209
WATERBURY   229
WILMINGTON   247
SOURCES   267

PREFACE

This book began in Baltimore. As weekend refugees from the bureaucracy-inspired neoclassical avenues of our home city, Washington, D.C., we began to explore the red brick neighborhoods and tumble-down industrial areas of that great port city just forty-five minutes to the north. By then, in the early 1970's, Baltimore was beginning to be discovered; now its old ethnic neighborhoods, waterfront revival, and fashionable newly rehabilitated blocks are the frequent subject of magazine and newspaper articles.

Our curiosity aroused, we broadened our explorations and discovered many smaller cities in the northeastern states with industrial roots and a contemporary pluckiness that led us to call them gritty cities. In the course of our travels we visited about forty such cities and decided to do a book on twelve that we liked best, where natural setting, historical events, and the people who came there combined to produce a special visual character that endures.

This is essentially a book of photographs and introductory essays that try to convey that special character. It is not an exhaustive treatise on the early years of urban industrial America or even a very detailed view of these industrial cities; for those interested in more information on the general subject or on any of the cities themselves, there is a list of the sources we used as well as a short bibliography of scholarly texts. Moreover, this book does not attempt to use the history and appearance of the gritty cities to make gloomy pronouncements on "urban decay"; too many cities like these have already been used as fodder for such invariably misaimed cannon.

If we have any thesis at all, it is the rather modest statement that such small cities do best when they grow and change by building on those things that gave them their character. Pat solutions imported via big-city consultants, no matter how bold and costly, never seem to succeed as well as carefully thought out approaches that use the unique mix of existing structures and neighborhoods, traditions and industries that comprise a city's legacy. A corollary is that to the extent these cities do look about for ideas, they should look more to each other's experiences and less to the nearby big cities. These cities probably cannot hope to recreate Boston's waterfront or Philadelphia's Society Hill, but their advantage of smaller size and scale can turn modest efforts into more immediate successes that have citywide impact.

In the course of putting together the photographs and text, we ran into many who were invaluable in helping us to understand what was going on in their towns. Among the most helpful were: Liz Kovert, Allentown Community Development Agency; Dan Church, *Bethlehem Globe Times*; Ross Yates, Lehigh University; Charles Brilvitch, Bridgeport Public Library; John Hyslop, Bridgeport Department of City Planning; Sal Policastro, Hoboken Municipal Home Improvement Program; Sal Santonello, Hoboken Community Development Department; John McCament and Ann Wilmoth, Lancaster City Planning Department; Earl Young, Lancaster Redevelopment Authority; Fred Bebisheimer, architect and former chairman of the Norwichtown Historic District; Jack Stokves, Paterson Department of Community Development; Mike Sposarsky, Paterson Public Library; Barry Kohl, Reading Chamber of Commerce; David Alexander, Reading Redevelopment Authority; Jane Silverman, consultant to the Trenton Department of City Planning; Tom and Kathleen McGuire, Hudson-Mohawk Industrial Gateway; Cornelius Maloney, *Waterbury Republican American*; Margaret Sargeant, Mattatuck Historical Society; Tom Johnson and Joey D'Orso, New Opportunities for Waterbury, Inc.; Carol Hoffecker, University of Delaware; and Judith Paine, Connecticut State Historical Commission.

These people as a group represent a refreshing contemporary commitment to urban living. They have chosen to help make these smaller cities places where living, working, and visiting can be attractive in the most modern terms amid many visually interesting reminders of the past.

We owe a special debt to John Alviti, an urban historian at Temple University, who read the manuscript and made many helpful suggestions for improving the historical accuracy of the section on the gritty cities in the industrial revolution. Special thanks are also due Don Canty, editor of the *AIA Journal*, who helped us develop our focus on the "gritty cities" and, in fact, came up with the name.

The maps are reproduced from the U.S. Geological Survey's 7½-minute series. The numbers on the maps correspond to the numbers of the photos in each chapter.

The research and photography for this book was funded in part by a grant from the National Endowment for the Arts.

M. E. P. and B. Mat.

GRITTY CITIES

INTRODUCING THE GRITTY CITIES

Tucked away on the backs of cough drop boxes, the bottoms of thermos jugs, and the labels of shirts you wear every day are found listed a number of not-so-faraway places with not very strange sounding names like Reading, Norwich, and Troy. These old manufacturing cities and nine others like them in the northeastern states—Allentown, Bethlehem, Bridgeport, Hoboken, Lancaster, Paterson, Trenton, Waterbury, and Wilmington —are the subject of this book.

In choosing cities to photograph for this book, we were drawn by the strong and consistent visual impressions that they conveyed. In some cities, it is the extraordinary uniformity of the housing stock that attracts; seen from above, Reading is a maze of rowhouse rooftops, with sawtooth patterns created by eaves and dormers that repeat hundreds of times up and down the hillsides all over the city. In other instances, the predominance of a single industry has left its mark on the visual character of the city; the steel mills of Bethlehem fill the valley of the Lehigh and tower above the soccer fields, church steeples, and historic burial grounds of the city. Other cities are places of striking contrasts; Trenton's stone colonial buildings are often wildly juxtaposed with neoclassical public buildings, nineteenth-century factories, and modern state government complexes. Finally, some cities' drawing card is nostalgia; the broad parks along the sea and wide residential streets of Bridgeport, for example, evoke not just things gone by, but a realization that cities can still be comfortable and attractive places to live.

Hoboken, Reading, and Lancaster are the three cities with the most uniformity in their housing stock, although they are otherwise quite different from each other.

Hoboken is a city of front stoops, iron railings, and walkups. Some streets cut through canyons of five story flats lining both sides far into the distance; other, quieter, streets are made up of smaller brownstones. The entire city of forty-five thousand is packed into a tight grid twelve by fourteen blocks, a crowded flat place between the steep palisades to the west and the Manhattan skyline across the Hudson. Hoboken is unique among its neighbors. To the north are a series of undefined communities atop the palisades, which curve out almost to the river and are visually leveled by high rise apartments along their crest. To the south Jersey City and Bayonne scatter out and lose themselves in rotting piers and long-abused marshes.

Reading looks like a working-class San Francisco; both cities are tied to a grid street pattern that obstinately ignores the steep hills everywhere. Downtown Reading shares the valley of the Schuylkill with the sprawling railroad yards. Stepping up the hills in all directions are hundreds and hundreds of rowhouses, all in neat lines that enhance their uniformity. Only closer inspection reveals the mottled texture created by stained-glass designs, ironwork porches, awnings, and permastone fronts. Where the rows give out deep forests begin and extend to the hilltops, one of which is capped by—of all things—a six-story pagoda.

Lancaster's look is created by blocks of colonial houses. Some are small enough to have emerged from nursery rhymes, but nearly all exude confidence they will take the next two centuries of use in stride. It is a market town that has the air of having grown up reluctantly and accepted industry with some measure of skepticism. Even today downtown is dominated by two old Amish farmers' markets.

Among the cities that derive their character most directly from a nineteenth-century legacy are Troy, the Iron City; Paterson, the Silk City; Bethlehem, the Steel City; and Waterbury, the Brass City.

The remnants of Troy's industries are spread along the Hudson from just above Albany to the falls of the Mohawk River and the locks of the modern counterpart of the Erie Canal. The city is blessed with a rich inheritance of elegant commercial and residential streets downtown, an elegance especially set off by the profusion of carved wooden bay windows and the use of shades of brown and other somber colors. Troy is so long north to south, and so narrow as it fits between the hills and the river, that most people who pass through on the major east-west routes get only about a thirty-second glimpse before they're gone.

In contrast to Troy's industrial sprawl, Paterson's mills are crowded around the Great Falls of the Passaic River, which drops over eighty feet into a rocky gorge of blackened roofs, steam clouds and smokestacks which still manage occasionally to belch smoke in this environmental era. The nearby neighborhoods have the tough, proud look of the breadwinners who have come home to them from the mills for over a century.

The steel mills in Bethlehem are so massive that, even though they are down low in the Lehigh Valley, they can be seen from almost anywhere, although the strange shapes reconfigure as you move from place to place. Worker housing scatters in attractive disarray over the hillsides beyond the mills, backing up from several directions into Lehigh University. Offsetting all this is an immaculately ordered historic district downtown, centered around the plain but ample stone meeting and residence halls of the first settlers, members of a communal Moravian sect.

Travelers to Waterbury usually recall two quite different landmarks—the tall graceful Siennese tower of the railroad station, now used as offices for the local newspapers, and Holy Land, a hillside devoted to a commercial reconstruction of most of Palestine in Biblical times, dominated by a spate of mighty crosses. But foremost, Waterbury is still known as the Brass City; the brass works, clock factories, and needle, pin and button works are still there, although some have been converted to new uses. It is a hilly city with a predominance of three-family wooden houses.

The cities of Wilmington, Norwich, and Trenton present strong visual contrasts within their boundaries; at the same time each contrasting element is internally very consistent so that the result is juxtaposition, rather than confusion.

Driving through on Interstate 95, Wilmington displays on one side a definite white-collar look, its impressive downtown skyline housing extensive banking and corporate interests and the world headquarters of the Du Pont chemical empire. On the other side, lining the hillsides to the west, are working-class neighborhoods arranged around churches that display in their architecture the ethnic origin of the residents. Two rivers frame the city; the Brandywine flows through beautiful parks and footpaths that connect the remains of old stone mills and raceways, while the Christina winds through marshes tangled with the debris of the shipbuilding and manufacturing concerns of a later era.

Norwich is another city whose rivers come from different directions and hold together the disparate elements. Colonial homes around a village green and along adjacent side streets have the look of old New England, but these give way quickly to an exuberant display of Victorian neighborhoods leading to the nineteenth-century town center down where all the rivers come together.

Trenton is a sadly neglected but rich collection of architectural remnants of two sharply contrasting eras, those of a colonial port city and an important manufacturing site. These sometimes impressive and sometimes touching vestiges surround and disrupt the sleek highrises which proclaim Trenton's modern role as the capital of America's eighth largest state. Industrial and historic districts, ethnic and elegant neighborhoods are strung incongruously along the intersecting bows of State Street from the northwest to northeast and Clinton Avenue from the northeast to the southeast.

The remaining two cities, Allentown and Bridgeport, look solid, prosperous and cheerful—the kinds of places where every American boy and girl not raised on a farm should have been brought up. Their attraction is in their ability to evoke this nostalgia.

Allentown displays countless blocks of plump brick rowhouses with white trim; corner stores and neighborhood schools and fire stations mix in here and there. Wooden awnings, often with elaborate trim and graceful curves, festoon the residential streets that lead into the downtown from the north, while more elegant Victorian neighborhoods come in from the west. The bustling retail center downtown has been transformed into an attractive mall with steel girders and plexiglass over the sidewalks as a unifying element.

Bridgeport is a seaside city with miles of public parks and beaches along Long Island Sound. The wooden houses are large and comfortable, with sea green the predominant color of the siding and shingles. Bridgeport is about midpoint in a string of wealthier and more ostentatious sibling cities that stretch from the bedroom suburbs of New York to New Haven; if anything, they help to set off Bridgeport as a wholesome working city.

A look at the past of the gritty cities explains much of what they are today. It is possible to identify many of the influences of location, early innovation and historical accident that worked together to create the visual character that has withstood decades of change. The outskirts of all the gritty cities display that familiar disarray of commercial strips, franchises, beltways and by-passes that have converted the environs of all American cities into humdrum predictability. Penetrating all this into the older parts of the cities takes you to what has been their past and what could be their future as special places to live.

The Gritty Cities in the Industrial Revolution

From about 1860 to about 1920 the development of industry in the United States fostered the growth of small cities. Before

1860 the few, very large, cities were more important as centers of trade and finance than of industry. New York had a population of over a million and Philadelphia half a million; other large cities such as Baltimore and Boston had populations of several hundred thousand. At mid-century, however, there were only twenty-six cities with populations of over 25,000 in the entire country.

By the turn of the century, the number of cities at least that big had increased sixfold; most of them were located in the leading manufacturing states. Even as the big cities grew bigger because of industrialization, many small towns had become middle-sized cities. This growth came to an end after World War I, when the large cities and their surrounding metropolitan areas once again took on the dominant role in industrial growth.

The particular twelve cities that are the subject of this book are infrequently mentioned in discussions of urbanization and industrialization in America. There is sufficient material, however, on the general phenomenon of the growth of small cities during the industrial revolution that it is possible to construct a framework for understanding the particular success of these cities in holding their own and even prospering against competition from the major metropolises during the years between 1860 and 1920.

Sometimes it was the availability of water power that gave advantages to the gritty cities for particular industries. As Allen Pred explains in his analysis of the location of industrial cities in this period, "Just as the mountain could not be moved to Mohammed, water power could not be moved to the city. The mechanized cotton textile industry could flourish in Waltham, Paterson or the Schuylkill suburbs [of Philadelphia] but not in Boston, New York, or Philadelphia proper." Of the twelve cities in this book, Norwich, Waterbury, Troy, Paterson, and Wilmington grew early in the nineteenth century with industries that used water power.

Transportation improved just enough in the period from about 1840 to 1880 to favor cities such as Reading, Allentown, Bethlehem, and Lancaster located on main transportation routes to ship finished products, but fairly close to coal beds and other raw materials. Troy's favorable location at the junction of the Erie Canal, the Hudson River and major railroads, combined with its excellent sources of water power, kept it competitive with bigger cities. Thus even small cities located on railroads, canals or navigable rivers had good access to sufficient markets to support industrial development at a scale that kept costs competitive. Especially in industries in which the value of a product was high compared to the cost of shipping it, businesses could develop almost as profitably in a small city as a large one.

There was no reason why energetic and innovative entrepreneurs couldn't succeed in the gritty cities. In the mid-nineteenth century Troy had a major role in the iron and steel industry due in part to two inventions: an incredibly productive horseshoe-making machine and an especially effective valve. Waterbury came from nowhere to a major role in both the brass and time keeping industries through the innovative manufacture of brass clocks and the famous Ingersoll Dollar Watch. Thomas Rogers made continual improvements in locomotive design that brought a major share of that industry to Paterson.

Small industrial cities located on good transportation routes could also attract industries relocating from elsewhere. They could compete with big cities in offering central industrial locations at land prices that were cheaper than such locations in the big cities and competitive with locations on their edges. Wilmington attracted shipbuilding and railroad car construction in the 1840's because good industrial sites cost less than comparable sites in Philadelphia or New York and transportation was nearly as good.

Those cities with early access to coal or water power got a head start in developing a pool of workers which were accustomed to manufacturing and in some cases familiar with particular industries. The tendency of immigrants to settle near relatives and acquaintances had the effect of ensuring the continuation of a steady flow of labor to a particular city. In two dramatic cases among the twelve cities, the immigrants actually brought with them skills which were essential in establishing the American capacity to compete with Europe. Thousands of silk workers emigrated from the English silk cities of Coventry and Macclesfield to the silk industry in Paterson. Skilled British workers also played a part in introducing sophisticated brass-making techniques into the embryonic Waterbury brass industry.

Most of the gritty cities had firms with national reputations. Four of the cities were among twelve in 1900 with over 20 percent of the production of a major industry. Troy produced over 85 percent of the nation's detachable collars and cuffs, Waterbury produced about 48 percent of the brassware and Paterson 24 percent of all silk and silk goods. Bridgeport captured 22 percent of all corset sales thanks in part to some clever innovations, one of which was to attach garters.

On average the twelve cities in this book grew rapidly, quintupling in size over the sixty years from 1860 to 1920. The accompanying table, however, shows that there were clear differences among the cities in the timing of growth. Lancaster, Norwich and Troy had achieved much of their eventual size by 1860 and grew fairly slowly after that. Allentown, Bethlehem, Bridgeport and Waterbury, on the other hand, grew fastest after 1890. All four of the latter prospered from sales to the United States government during World War I.

Despite their impressive growth, however, the gritty cities did not become big cities. The existing large cities, such as New York, Philadelphia and Baltimore continued to attract industry and became even bigger, doubling or tripling in size from 1860 to 1900.

	Population in:	
	1860	1900
New York	1,174,799	3,437,202
Baltimore	212,418	508,957
Pittsburgh	77,233	451,512

In the same period, a few strictly manufacturing cities—Pittsburgh, Cleveland and Detroit—whose economies were very like those of the gritty cities entered the ranks of dominant large

GRITTY CITY POPULATIONS   1860–1920

	Populations as of:		
	1860	1890	1920
EARLY GROWTH			
Lancaster	17,603	32,011	53,150
Norwich	14,048	16,156	22,304
Troy	39,235	60,956	72,013
LATE GROWTH			
Allentown	8,025	25,228	73,502
Bethlehem	2,866	17,094	50,358
Bridgeport	13,299	48,866	143,555
Waterbury	10,004	28,646	91,646
CONTINUOUS GROWTH			
Hoboken	9,662	43,648	68,166
Paterson	19,586	73,347	135,875
Reading	23,162	58,661	107,784
Trenton	17,228	57,458	119,289
Wilmington	21,258	61,431	110,168
AVERAGE	16,331	43,625	87,323

cities by skillfully achieving preeminence in such industries as steel that had national markets.

By the end of World War I, a series of changes had taken place in the American economy which drastically reduced the role of small and middle-sized cities and gave the clear edge to the big cities. The most important shift took place in the type of manufactured goods being produced. Goods produced in the 1870's, such as horseshoes, corsets, stoves, and steel rails, were directly usable in an agrarian economy. With rapid industrialization, capital goods became the more valuable manufactured goods; steel companies, for example, shifted production from steel rails to structural steel. A big city location was a definite advantage in marketing these goods to other manufacturers.

At the same time, firms selling to the emerging nationwide markets were benefited by cheaper railroad freight rates as a result of technical and managerial improvements; rates dropped over 40 percent between 1882 and 1900. Furthermore, improved communications through telegraph and telephone encouraged the consolidation of firms and the establishment of their headquarters in big cities close to the sources of big capital. Finally, the development of trucking gave manufacturing firms a wider choice of locations near the big cities. Trucks were used to transport goods to railroads and ports even though they did not become a long-distance shipping alternative until after World War II.

On average there has been virtually no growth in the gritty cities since 1920. Although four of the cities—Allentown, Bethlehem, Norwich and Waterbury—have increased substantially, five others—Troy, Wilmington, Reading, Hoboken and Trenton—have lost population. In all cases, however, the populations of the metropolitan areas surrounding these cities have increased many times since 1920. Allentown and Bethlehem, for example, are both part of the fast-growing Lehigh Valley metropolitan area. Troy is part of a similar multi-city area that includes Albany and Schenectady.

In the South and Southwest, cities large and small have been able to tap some of the wealth created by manufacturing and commerce on their outskirts by annexing surrounding townships and counties. Since the 1920's this course of action for cities of all sizes in the Northeastern states has been severely restricted by rigid laws prohibiting annexation except under very difficult conditions (such as explicit approval by state legislatures). Thus the gritty cities share with the larger Northeastern cities the financial problems created by the shrinking of the industrial base within their boundaries and commercial as well as industrial site competition from the suburbs.

As they come into the late twentieth century these twelve cities must cope with both the physical legacy of the important industrial role they served until 1920 and the economic problems created by the decline in that role over the last half century. A surprising number have risen to the challenge to turn that legacy from a liability to an asset.

The Mills

Horseshoes and parlor cars, sewing machines and straight pins made in the gritty cities were almost all manufactured in red brick mills, many of which are still standing.

Some of the mill buildings were deliberately designed to be beautiful and to reflect the good taste of the owner. The Ponemah mill, built in 1873 in Norwich, looks more like a chateau than a factory filled with thousands of looms. Harmony Mill Number 3 in Cohoes near Troy sports mansard roofs on quadruple towers topped with ornate ironwork.

Most of the mill buildings, however, were designed in a more practical mode to house manufacturing efficiently and to protect the owner's investment from loss. The early gunpowder mills of the Du Ponts, for example, exhibit three heavy stone walls. The roof and a fourth wall facing out over the river, however, are built of flimsy wood, to direct any explosions up and away from adjacent mills.

For the most part the nineteenth-century mills and factories in these cities were of brick and reflect the principle of "slow-burning mill construction" then being worked out. Less expensive than completely fireproof buildings, these wooden frame brick structures would burn for long periods before collapse, thus allowing time to get employees and valuable goods out and perhaps even extinguish the fire before all was consumed. Wide truss spans provided flexible space with minimal columns; arched lintels and brick cornices gave added strength to the supporting structures. All these details, beside serving purely functional purposes, are also attractive to today's eye, as modern American architectural style moves away from an era of unremitting plainness and uniformity.

The physical legacy left by industrial development was not confined to the mill buildings themselves. The most generous and broad-minded of the entrepreneurs used their wealth to create monuments to themselves in the form of such public facilities as parks, schools, hospitals, and institutes of higher education. Excellent technical schools were set up in three of the cities by wealthy industrialists. The earliest of these was Rensselaer Polytechnic Institute in Troy, which was founded in 1823. Stevens Tech in Hoboken was established in 1869 by the family of the city's founder, an ingenious inventor of machinery in his own right, while railroad money established Lehigh University in Bethlehem.

Some cities were especially fortunate in tapping such business wealth. The Du Ponts put their chemical profits to use in constructing the public schools of Wilmington; the Bancrofts built the city's parks with cotton textile wealth. Funds for the design and partial endowment of Allentown's extensive park system came from a cement manufacturer, General Henry Clay Trexler.

Not all cities, however, were so lucky in their entrepreneurs. Jacob Rogers, who took over the locomotive works in Paterson from his father, was asked to donate a small strip of his land for part of the site of a hospital. As recounted in a memoir by Charles Shriner, an acquaintance, Mr. Rogers refused and added, "What do I want to do with your hospital? I have enough money to keep me out of it and my friends too. I do not owe the hospital nor Paterson either, anything at all." He proceeded to leave his entire estate to the Metropolitan Museum in New York City, a place he had visited only once. Paterson, for its size, is in fact remarkably poorly endowed with parks and cultural institutions.

Beginning in about 1920, the red brick mills, from which the wealth of the gritty cities was created, began a long slide into obsolescence. One by one, they were downgraded in industrial value and were sold or rented to less profitable firms or abandoned altogether.

The old underutilized mill buildings often provided the path of least resistance for freeways through the cities. Both Waterbury and Bridgeport saw major old industrial areas cleared out for new interstate highways to facilitate travel and commerce.

In Paterson, however, the highway builders were stopped cold. It was the threat of destruction of the old silk mills below the falls that galvanized public opinion to stop the extension of Highway 20 on its illogical route north to nowhere. The entire mill district is now on the National Register of Historic Landmarks. Although continuation of the highway project seems impossible at this point, the Department of Transportation still owns a number of the old mills which it had bought earlier, and is allowing them to fall victim to decay, arson, and neglect.

Of course, some manufacturing concerns remain in these cities. Aside from Du Pont and Bethlehem Steel, Mack Trucks in Allentown, Maxwell House Coffee in Hoboken, and Ludens in Reading are good examples. However, other major companies that began in the gritty cities maintain only small-scale operations, often in the shadow of the underused mills. Among these are Arrow Shirts in Troy and Timex in Waterbury. In many cases, the early manufacturing firms have been bought out by larger companies or conglomerates. Of Waterbury's big three brass companies, only one, Scovill, is still locally owned. Because in such cases decisions to modernize or close a plant are subject to the vagaries of overall corporate planning, local residents hold their breath when firms are bought out by non-local interests.

Some old mills continue to house one or more small low-budget manufacturing businesses such as textiles, dye-making, or machine tool shops—the kinds of enterprises that are very vulnerable to changes in the minimum wage or environmental or safety regulations. Owners have difficulty doing anything beyond minimum upkeep of the old buildings. Furthermore, economic survival mandates that the industries be far less labor intensive than they once were. An old mill in Paterson houses one of two firms in the nation which still produce silk ribbon. The company has stayed in business because its inventive owner has devised ways to automate the machinery so that it can run virtually unattended all night. Where hundreds of workers were once needed, fewer than a dozen suffice today.

New owners have renovated some of the old factories for modern use. Ursula of Switzerland, a woman's knitwear manufacturer, has converted an old textile mill near Troy into colorful design studios. Bryant Electric, a subsidiary of Westinghouse in Bridgeport, has carefully cleaned and restored an old brick factory for manufacturing.

Troy and Paterson have both become centers for the emerging study of industrial archeology, a discipline with a good chance of spreading in coming years to all the gritty cities. Supported by the Smithsonian Institution and state governments, teams of engineers, architects, and historians have begun to excavate and document the earliest structures and technologies in the Troy-Cohoes area and in the Paterson historic mill district. Funds are being sought for the reconstruction of spillways and water wheels and the provision of walking tours of important historic sites. Similar restoration work was done years ago in Wilmington when the Du Pont family funded the excavation and restoration of their early mills and the formation of the Hagley Museum of nineteenth-century industrial history. The current movement broadens that early effort to other cities and supports it with government funds.

The renewed interest in the historical importance of these industrial buildings has added fuel to a general effort to find new uses for them in the interests of making cities of all sizes more attractive and livable. Contributing to this "adaptive use" movement have been the need for energy conservation (some of the solid old mills come off very well in comparison to newer construction), the focus the bicentennial celebration gave to local celebrations of history, the renewed interest in finding one's roots, and the growing dissatisfaction with the design and siting of new development on the outskirts of cities. Spurred on by the success of the conversion of an old chocolate factory to Ghiradelli Square in San Francisco and the use of old lofts as artists' studios in Soho in Manhattan, a number of similar efforts are underway in the gritty cities.

The Corset Factory in Bridgeport is now a series of snappy boutiques, factory outlet stores, and restaurants. The Keuffel and Esser precision instrument factory was converted into an elegant apartment building in Hoboken. Paterson has tried with limited success to attract artists to its factory lofts, and it has already located one public and two private elementary schools in renovated mill space. The old Arrow Shirt Bleachery, on an island in the Hudson near Troy, has been taken over by the State of New York, which is converting it into a center of studios, workshops, and reconstruction projects for historic preservation.

Factories in the midst of these cities are no longer important in American manufacturing. However, the architectural legacy left from what was once the remarkably important role played by mills in these and other small cities is lending flavor to contemporary efforts to design new forms for commerce and urban living.

The Neighborhoods

For the first half of the nineteenth century, what industry there was in the gritty cities developed mostly within an English-speaking society, although the Pennsylvania cities, Allentown, Lancaster, and Reading, all had a German flavor from the Pennsylvania Dutch that settled there. Bethlehem was a special case, since it was founded by a group of Moravians who refused to sell land to outsiders until 1845. The Moravians and their church and college still dominate the cultural life of the town. The families descended from early settlers—such as the Quakers in Wilmington—often ended up as the upper class in the society from the mere fact of their long residence, although the boundary with less socially prominent families was not always distinct. As Henry Canby, a member of an early Quaker family, wrote in a memoir of late nineteenth-century life in Wilmington (quoted in Carol Hoffecker's history of Wilmington), "As for the plain people, they were the pit from which we were dug. Most of Us had relatives among them . . . . The difference between them and Us was a subtle one of manners and tradition, chiefly tradition, for our manners were not always good."

The flavor of early settlement survives today in the names on the earliest gravestones and the family names associated with the oldest residential architecture. After this period most of the gritty cities underwent overwhelming changes in cultural atmosphere as they were transformed by three waves of immigrants seeking work in their mills: from Northern Europe beginning in the mid-nineteenth century; from Eastern Europe and the Mediterranean through World War I; and, beginning in the nineteen sixties, from Puerto Rico and South America. These migrations affected the twelve cities quite differently.

The first wave of immigration sent Germans to Allentown, Reading, and Lancaster as part of a larger flow of "Pennsylvania Dutch" (Germans). A hilly residential section of Lancaster, largely settled by Germans, is still referred to as "Cabbage Hill." Germans were much more conspicuous in Hoboken, comprising nearly 25 percent of a population of 44,000 in 1890. Hoboken had German newspapers, clubs, music halls and beer gardens with such names as Germania Garden and Harmonia Hall.

Irish immigrants went to four cities in large numbers: to Troy where they were 15 percent of the population in 1890, and to Paterson, Bridgeport, and Waterbury. Regardless of their numbers, however, Irish immigrants came to dominate the politics of several of the gritty cities.

The second wave of immigration, from Southern and Eastern Europe from the 1880's to 1914 was particularly felt in Waterbury, Bridgeport, Hoboken and Paterson. These four cities were comprised of about one-third foreign born and another third of foreign parentage in 1920. Trenton, Norwich, Wilmington and Troy all had substantial but smaller groups of immigrants. Italians were by far the biggest group in almost all these cities, leaving a legacy of Italian restaurants and coffeehouses everywhere. In cities like Wilmington, it was during the second wave of immigration that distinct ethnic neighborhoods began to be formed. There are still Italian neighborhoods in Wilmington (Little Italy), Waterbury (Town Plot Hill) and Trenton (Chambersburg).

The Eastern European groups, smaller in numbers than the Italians, were attracted to particular cities: Hungarians to Bridgeport, Trenton, and Bethlehem; Poles to Wilmington,

Paterson, Norwich and Reading; Lithuanians to Waterbury and Russians to Bridgeport. Most of these groups remained heavily concentrated in particular sections. Some of these neighborhoods are nearly intact to this day. Browntown and Hedgeville, Polish neighborhoods off Maryland Avenue in Wilmington, have survived to see young Polish couples choose their family rowhouses over the suburbs.

Spanish-speaking groups, the most recent wave of immigration, have also been attracted to particular cities. Hoboken has been settled by Puerto Ricans while Paterson has drawn Spanish-speaking people from South American countries as well as from Puerto Rico.

Even where neighborhoods are not dominated by single groups, there is a feeling of ethnicity to many of the residential neighborhoods of the gritty cities. Little neighborhood barbershops, coffee houses and flower shops appear right in the middle of blocks of houses, many of them with signs in Italian, Polish or Spanish. The cultural origins of churches are often clearly recognizable: Orthodox onion domes, tile-roofed Italian or heavily Gothic Eastern European.

In a few cases, a large share of the housing for immigrant and other workers was built by the mill owners. Up the hill from the Harmony Mills near Troy still stand several hundred units of plain but attractive rowhouses and duplexes in brick and frame. Company housing lines the streets near the Ponemah mills near Norwich, as well. There are other smaller groups of company housing such as that built next to the Bancroft mills in Wilmington. A mixture of public and corporate construction helped to house the 40 percent increase in Bridgeport's population that accompanied industrialization during World War I.

Elsewhere, housing to accommodate the fast population growth in these cities was built by private developers, although few details of how they operated remain. We know, for example, that much of Wilmington's worker housing was built by a single developer, Joshua T. Heald. Many of Reading's rows, on the other hand, were built by workers' savings and loan societies. Rowhouses in Allentown, with their scores of similar porches and turrets, and Hoboken, with their even cornice lines, have the look of large-scale development. So do the large wooden houses in Bridgeport that city officials estimate form half the city's housing stock. The coming in the mid-nineteenth century of widely read architectural design books and mail-order ornaments made up-to-date architectural fashions available to all cities and gave a wide range of ideas to local builders and craftsmen, from which they developed their own applications of style.

There does not appear to have been a stained glass factory in Reading, yet over half of the rowhouses there, including the smallest, were given stained glass windows by their builders. Hoboken walkups, on the other hand, compete with each other in elaborate iron balustrades. Troy builders added ornate rectangular bay windows to almost all townhouses regardless of original style. Allentown rowhouses reflect a fad for ornate wooden awnings over the doorways. Wilmington's duplexes are covered in gray fish-scale shingles, while Waterbury boasts wooden three deckers with asymetrical tiers of columned porches.

Colors, another accident of fashion, give a distinctive feel to some of these cities. The fat wooden houses of Bridgeport are overwhelmingly pastel: pink, blue and especially sea green. Trenton rowhouses in some sections come in intense shades of deep green and red. Troy's streets are in elegant earthy colors: olive, chocolate, mustard and rust, while Allentown's rowhouses are almost all red brick with white trim. And in many of Waterbury's triple-deckers each floor is painted a different color.

Housing for the more affluent, while less numerous than working class housing, has been important in setting style in the gritty cities. The tone is simple elegance in Lancaster, derived from the townhouses built by wealthy residents in the eighteenth and early nineteenth centuries. The simplicity of the eighteenth-century Moravian architecture in Bethlehem is even more powerful. It was built to house the founding religious sect, which practiced communal living well into the nineteenth century.

Norwich, on the other hand, specializes in ornate styles for nineteenth-century detached frame houses, offering beautifully kept examples of Greek and Gothic Revival, Italianate, Queen Anne, shingle, Italian villa and more. Waterbury, Bridgeport and Troy all have smaller sections of notable frame Victorians.

In most cities the housing is in better shape than the fashionable lament of urban decay would lead one to expect. In some cases what initially appears to be decay later turns out to be planners' blight, long-awaited destruction for urban renewal or for a highway. The fact that such artificially blighted areas are often found near paths taken by visitors, near downtown, or along major throughroutes, have contributed to an image of far more widespread physical deterioration of housing than actually exists. One of the twelve cities, Reading, has had so little blight that city officials estimate that there are no more than fifty abandoned houses in the entire city. Lancaster, Norwich, Troy, Bethlehem, and Allentown are examples of other cities with few areas of visible blight. Only Paterson, Waterbury, Trenton, and Bridgeport have blighted areas large enough to pose a major challenge to city revitalization efforts.

It is no coincidence that three of the four cities with major problems of blight have a very high proportion of frame houses. The big wooden houses in all the cities have had the hardest time surviving. Poor maintenance can lead more quickly to visible deterioration than the same neglect of brick or stone buildings. The size of these houses makes them difficult to keep up as the single-family residences they were originally intended to be; even owner-occupants often must rely on tenants to offset the high heating and maintenance costs. Moreover, neighborhoods of large wooden houses can more quickly end up as a clutter of parking lots, new garden apartment buildings and a few remaining houses than can neighborhoods of rowhouses, where knocking down a single house is neither structurally easy nor financially lucrative.

The biggest, most ornate Victorian houses have survived best where they have been converted from single family residential use. Many beauties, sadly, can survive only in the macabre form of funeral parlors. In some cities, such as Waterbury and Bridgeport, the fancy Victorian neighborhoods have been zoned for professional and institutional use. Law partnerships and medical groups are doing a valuable service in keeping the porches, gables, and bay windows of these old houses in good condition.

Brick and stone cities, such as Lancaster and Troy, have been fortunate in that housing more than a century old has remained solid and usable until the 1970's, when fashion is beginning to attract private residential investment back into the cities. Lancaster is several years into a private residential back-to-the-cities boom. Blocks and blocks of rowhouses have the Williamsburg lamps and oversized house numbers that signal renovation. Troy is a few years behind Lancaster but has good prospects of undergoing a similar large-scale private redevelopment. Allentown is at a still earlier stage. Trenton and Wilmington both have small areas of renovated old rowhouses.

Because private renovation is largely a matter of fashion, the role of neighborhood self-consciousness has been important in creating the right social climate. Lancaster has an active historic district association working among the blocks of most distinguished houses, while the city government has worked with neighborhood groups in most of the other areas of the city. The Allentown city government deliberately tried to create strong citizen groups in every neighborhood; at their best, the groups have actively encouraged renovation by residents. Designation as an historic district stimulated the formation of a similarly active neighborhood association in Troy. City officials in Reading hope that a planned historic district on either side of the main square will lend coherence to an area of some of the more attractive housing in the city.

Government-subsidized loans and grants to homeowners for renovation have played a minor role in many cities but an enormous role in one of them—Hoboken. Hoboken has been able to put a variety of federal and state housing subsidy programs to use in a locally-conceived program for renovating owner-occupied and multi-family housing. About a third of the city's housing units will have been renovated by 1980. Bridgeport and Allentown assist low-income homeowners in a similar manner, but on a much smaller scale. Urban homesteading, one of the most imaginative ways to attack housing blight, began in Wilmington and has spread to many other cities. Housing units owned by the city have been given away to homeowners, who are legally committed to bring them up to building code standards on a fair timetable and to live in them.

Prospects for continued private development of urban housing are good, although long-term commitments by those with children are threatened by the shaky situation of most of the city school systems. Nonetheless, increasing construction and energy costs as well as a revival of the taste for urban living combine to make older urban structures increasingly competitive with the suburbs in most of the gritty cities.

Downtown

Nineteenth-century industrialization gave new impetus to boosterism in the gritty cities. The art of photography was flourishing, and prominent citizens commissioned photo albums of their downtowns, residential streets, parks, schools and hospitals. The photographs show prosperous (if often muddy) downtowns with elaborate public buildings, department stores, specialty stores, restaurants, and hotels.

Today it is the public life of the commercial downtowns that has caused most of the struggle and controversy in the gritty cities, since they symbolize the city's health and help support the city's tax base. These once-flourishing areas have been threatened by the same forces that have undermined commercial downtowns in much larger cities. Difficult annexation laws have confined such cities as Lancaster and Wilmington to no more than a fifth of the population of their metropolitan areas; suburbs can reap what would be the city's taxes and evade its problems. Within the last five years enclosed suburban shopping malls have opened up a few miles from downtown in virtually all the cities. With their plazas, fountains and pseudo-urban atmosphere created among acres of parking, they have been enormously threatening to downtown department stores and shops. Fears of crime and congested streets, in some cases justified, have further weakened the downtown areas at the expense of the suburbs.

Despite their economic troubles, the downtowns of many gritty cities are fun to look at. Many buildings boast ornate facades with carved faces and brackets and hooded lintels. On the first floors, to be sure, modern alterations and obtrusive signs detract from the architecture above.

Public buildings also reflect the era of greater prosperity in these cities. Paterson produced an impressive array, including three county courthouses—one Greek, one Flemish (originally the Post Office), and one functional modern—and a Beaux Arts city hall. Other cities also have fine collections of public architecture. Much of the charm of downtown Norwich derives from its marvelous town hall, the only structure that seems to sit straight on its irregular hilly square. Lancaster has a row of fine public buildings on Duke Street, ending in an impressive sand colored early Greek Revival county courthouse at King Street. In Waterbury, an imposing set of city, county and federal buildings, from Cass Gilbert recreations of other eras to tasteful modern, live together along the broad street which leads to the Siennese tower on the McKim, Meade and White railroad station.

The last decade has brought much new public architecture to the gritty cities as they have sought to reestablish their pride and their identity on the one hand, and to fill in the vacant lots of their urban renewal mistakes on the other. Notably good results have been obtained in Troy, where the ultramodern lines of the new City Hall mesh surprisingly well with the surrounding Victorian storefronts, in part because the new building is kept at human scale. More extensive but in equally good taste are the buildings in Bethlehem's new civic center, which combines modern lines with gray tones to reflect the stone Moravian buildings across the street and down the block. The complex, although prominently located on a bluff overlooking the Lehigh River and the steel mills, is unobtrusive to the historic district that surrounds it on the other three sides. Lancaster has a modern annex next door to its Greek Revival county courthouse;

while normally this might be an alarming clash of styles, careful choice of materials and a modest but attractive design allow the new building to fit in smoothly with the old. But it is Trenton that has seen the most of new public architecture, as the state government has expanded into complexes of ungainly office buildings between downtown and the Delaware River.

Restaurants and hotels lead a precarious existence in many of the gritty cities, but they are important symbols in the successful downtowns. Where they survive and prosper they make their cities seem well established.

The place to find the best meals in Paterson, Trenton, and Hoboken are the old-fashioned Jewish deli's, Irish and Italian taverns, and Latin American cafes with formica topped tables. But the movement to comfortable contemporary quiche-and-salad restaurants has reached a number of the cities. Such places can be found off a back alley in downtown Lancaster, in a converted Victorian rowhouse in Troy, and in an elegant old apartment hotel in Allentown. There are old family restaurants that have served fine food for decades in almost all the cities. One famous restaurant in Reading specializes in mushroom dishes; the place closes down in August and September while four generations of the owner's family hunt wild mushrooms as far away as Ontario.

Downtown hotels range from excellent to virtually non-existent. For pure elegance and traditional good taste, it is difficult to beat the Hotel Bethlehem and the Hotel Du Pont, both subsidized by their corporate owners to provide first-class lodging for their visitors. The Hotel Brunswick in Lancaster is operated by the resort subsidiary of the corporation built by a local candy store owner who made good, Milton Hershey. And Norwich is served by the colonial Leffingwell Inn in Old Norwichtown.

In Waterbury and Allentown the most fashionable old hotels have been converted to offices and apartments. In both cases there are new franchise hotels downtown to take their place with less charm but more efficiency. Bridgeport, Trenton, and Troy also have new downtown hotels built by the national chains, but in Reading a similar effort failed. And there are still no good hotels at all in Paterson or Hoboken. The fate of downtown hotels in some cities is hopelessly tangled up in urban renewal projects, which have also had bad effects on the survival of most downtown department stores.

The role of local government planning and renewal agencies in the downtowns of the gritty cities reflects the current confusion at a major turning point in the philosophical approach of government to solving urban problems—a shift from a basic desire to tear everything down and start all over again to a commitment to maximize the use and reuse of existing structures.

Some cities still bear the scars of the demolition-mad phase of the fifties and sixties. Wilmington's empty area comprised twenty-six continuous city blocks that are only now beginning to be filled in around the edges. Reading still has twelve empty city blocks right in the middle of downtown. Paterson and Waterbury also have extensive vacant land.

For the moment, these empty lots help to satisfy an appetite for parking spaces that would astonish a visitor from a big city accustomed to overcrowded garage parking and high rates. Not content with using most of the vacant blocks for surface parking, revenue-short city governments have in many cases built parking garages at the first opportunity, even though on-street parking and surface lots are only partly used. The evident rationale for this excess of parking is to allay the fears of prospective suburban shoppers that they might need to walk through crime-ridden streets from a parking space to the store they seek.

Two cities—Bridgeport and Lancaster—which have essentially completed textbook programs to tear down large sections of downtown and rebuild it, indicate the limits of the standard renewal approach. Bridgeport built its own enclosed shopping mall, Lafayette Plaza, to compete with suburban malls. Offering a massive parking garage right next door and two department stores, the Plaza is holding its own. Bridgeport's large population of about 150,000 and the easy access to the mall from the Connecticut Turnpike have been the conditions that have enabled it to make good.

Lancaster's new construction is visually more striking than Bridgeport's, but it has had serious economic troubles. A new Lancaster branch of Allentown's highly-respected Hess department store lasted only a year; the space is now a factory outlet on one floor. During the same period of Hess's unsuccessful entry into downtown Lancaster retailing, two of the three other department stores also went under. The Hilton chain moved out of the new hotel and sold their interest to Hershey. A block of stores on the west side of the new complex were unrented until taken over as office space for part of Armstrong Cork's headquarters. The east side is only now being developed, after standing vacant for three years.

This experience has led Lancaster's city officials to decide on a new and more realistic combination of economic roles for their downtown: to focus on office buildings, middle income housing through private restoration of nearby neighborhoods, and specialty stores. In effect, Lancaster has decided to leave general retailing to the suburbs. Nearby Reading, with its still-empty blocks, is not oblivious to the lesson of Lancaster and has decided on a similar strategy for its own new construction. A new office building is expected to open in 1978; its first two floors will house such specialized enterprises as a French restaurant and a cooking school. But Reading is also taking heed from Lancaster's costly half-occupied new buildings and proceeding cautiously, testing the market at each step. It promises to be some years before the empty blocks are filled.

More flexible sources of federal money to cities in the seventies have encouraged more innovative ways of breathing life back into downtowns. The Housing and Community Development Act of 1974 replaced a number of old categorical grant programs, including urban renewal, with a single block grant to cities. This produced two immediate benefits. First, local government was given more leeway in choosing projects for funding. Second, for the first time citizens could clearly pin down who was responsible for renewal and redevelopment decisions because City Hall, and not Washington or some remote federal regional office, had the legal duty to make the choices. The result was that much more of the funds began to flow to neighborhood improvement and small-scale efforts to build on existing resources downtown, and much less went to grand schemes and wholesale demolition.

Two other new federal laws have proved beneficial to these cities for a similar reason. The Local Public Works Act and the Comprehensive Employment Training Act were both enacted by Congress to meet immediate needs for construction activity and jobs. Both included very short timetables for applications by local governments, which meant almost no time for project planning. As a result, cities had to draw on what was available in the way of resources and on projects on the shelf and ready to go. This often meant that projects for reuse or adaptive use of existing structures got funded, since over the years feasibility studies for such projects had often been prepared with small grants from preservation groups, the National Endowment for the Arts, or other sources. The large-scale traditional renewal projects, by contrast, were often tied up in the planning process or in acquisition problems. Thus, these two federal programs are helping with such projects as the conversion of the Rogers Locomotive Works to a museum in Paterson; the reuse of an old high school in Troy as a county office building; the development of a medical and community center out of an old clock works in Waterbury; and the conversion of the Hoboken ferry terminal into a shopping arcade.

Another solution to downtown's economic problems has had only mixed results. The expensive and often disruptive way to improve the attractiveness of commercial blocks has been to block traffic with a pedestrian mall. Wilmington's six-block mall, centered on the ornate old Opera House, is fairly bustling. Reading's two-block mall, however, fills a street so wide that a pedestrian gets lost among the potted trees and street furniture. Trenton and Bethlehem both compromised with shorter malls that cause traffic confusion and congestion without creating a significant change in atmosphere. Paterson's attempt at a one block mall doesn't obstruct traffic because it is a covered side street that forms the nucleus of a group of fruit, fish and meat markets.

Improvements in sidewalks and facades that do not disrupt traffic have been visually successful and much less financially risky than pedestrian malls. The most ambitious effort is a half-mile set of iron and curved plastic-covered walkways in Allentown. More modest attempts at improving sidewalk appearances are also underway. Waterbury has rebuilt several blocks of sidewalk in an inviting brick and cement pattern and added pine tree planters. The results are more elegant than the more typical profusion of plastic and metal kiosks, benches and arcades.

Improving store facades themselves is often a delicate matter, since the individual owners may not think in terms of the overall effect. Lancaster has used some of its community development block grant money to hire a design advisor to work with the Greater Lancaster Corporation, an association of downtown merchants. The city planning department has produced a beautifully illustrated guide to renovating commercial buildings that is being distributed to all commercial property owners. To date only a few cities, such as Troy and Hoboken, have developed programs to financially assist store owners with renovation or facade restoration.

Both Reading and Bridgeport illustrate one way for cities to recapture retail markets without significant public costs. In the last five years private investors in Reading have developed a booming business in factory outlet sales in old mills. There is even a factory outlet for Givenchy designer-label women's clothes. Bridgeport has added a sophisticated touch by combining specialty boutiques with the factory outlet stores in its recycled old mill, the Corset Factory.

Using mill buildings for factory outlets is an effective way to take advantage of the natural image of a factory town. Space for such stark retail uses can be renovated much more cheaply than for almost any other use and yet need not be dreary. The best of Reading's outlets are decorated with banners and wall paintings in bright colors. Factory outlets also appeal to lower-income residents of the town. Paterson plans to create a complex of craft workshops and boutiques in one of its old mills. A well conceived complement of factory outlets would add bustle to the mill area and attract customers to everything there.

It is clear that successful solutions to downtown decay must be crafted to fit the resources and realistic economic prospects of each city. For decades the two parts of Bethlehem on either side of the Lehigh River had better street and trolley connections to nearby Allentown than to each other. The result is a commercial district in Allentown that has traditionally served a wide area. For Allentown to build on that tradition makes good sense. For Bethlehem to try to compete with Allentown's department stores would be wasteful and could work to the detriment of both cities. Instead, Bethlehem would probably do better to build its commercial life around the tourists in the old Moravian district on the north side of the river, and the students at Lehigh University on the south side. Similarly, Lancaster's decision to treat downtown as a service center for office workers and residents of restored nearby neighborhoods is a better bet for the future than to try to compete with suburban shopping centers. Bridgeport and Waterbury, on the other hand, are commercial centers for the surrounding regions and both have good highway access to downtown; for these the future might well lie in keeping intact an attractive retail downtown designed to appeal to a wide range of customers.

The need for such sensible strategies also applies to the overall role the gritty cities choose to play in coming decades. While downtown revival will be important to all of them, the interplay and relative importance of downtown, industry, and neighborhoods will—and should—vary, to take full advantage of each city's potential. Hoboken, Lancaster, and Troy have already become bedroom cities for affluent commuters to New York, Harrisburg, and Albany, respectively; the trend in real estate prices in all three cities indicates a solid basis for growth in that direction. Trenton and Wilmington both have enough of a white collar work force downtown to justify major efforts to make living in the city fashionable for those who work there.

This is not to say that there is an easy solution in every case. In some cities, major national economic issues lie at the base of future prospects; for Paterson an infusion of new investment to solve unemployment seems critical, while Bethlehem needs stability in the steel industry.

Compared to bigger cities, the gritty cities remain places where traditions are better remembered, the scale is more human, and urban problems seem less intractable. Perhaps these cities, which served the industrial revolution so well between 1860 and 1920, are entering a period when their attributes are once again valued, now less for their economic advantages and more for their basic livability.

Whether this happens will depend in part on how well they have learned the lessons of the decades of stagnation. To some extent this must be an introspective process—to identify and build upon what is unique in each city. To some extent the experiences of other cities should also prove valuable—not those of big cities, which are often emulated but seldom relevant, but those of other smaller cities. Lancaster's experiences with renewal and its decisions about the future of downtown should be noted by the other gritty cities, as should Hoboken's and Wilmington's successful housing rehabilitation programs. What Troy and Paterson have begun in industrial archeology should be of interest and value to Waterbury, Trenton, and other places where industrialization began early.

If these cities make it into an era of renewed value and purpose, they offer much. They are powerful visual reminders of our history, its exuberance, and its struggles. They offer human-scale opportunities for urban living, and they house treasures—ornate courthouses, grand movie houses, broad Victorian avenues, rows of stained glass windows—that enrich the lives of all who pass by.

ALLENTOWN

ALLENTOWN'S BEGINNING HAD NEITHER THE RELIGIOUS
fervor of the founding of nearby Bethlehem by the Moravians
nor the profiteering fervor of the founding of Paterson by Alexander Hamilton and his associates. Allentown's beginning was
eminently respectable. The former mayor of Philadelphia and
Chief Justice of the Supreme Court of Pennsylvania, Judge William Allen, laid out a grid in the forest in 1762 in the expectation
that from that act would arise a city.

Modeled on the plan of Philadelphia, the grid was organized
around the main streets intersecting in a central square; today
these have become Hamilton Avenue and Seventh Street con-
verging on the Soldiers and Sailors Monument. The combination of a well-planned grid on a well-drained plateau some
seventy-five feet above two creeks feeding into the Lehigh
River fostered the development of a quite pleasant but undra-
matic city.

Judge William Allen was so respectable that he returned to
England rather than support the Revolution, leaving the further
development of the grid in the woods to his patriot son, James,
who unfortunately died soon after in 1778. Although the borough was officially named Northampton, it became known as
"Mr. Allen's little town," and Allentown became its official

. Wooden awnings on Ninth Street

name in 1838. The settlement of the town was so dominated by Pennsylvania Germans that until 1817 the only newspaper was in German. German could still be heard in the streets until recent years.

Despite its loyalist origins, the town earned Revolutionary kudos when two Allentown citizens transported the Liberty Bell from Philadelphia to protect it from being melted down by the British. The Bell was kept under the floor of the Zion Reformed Church for nearly a year. The descendants of the two men squabbled for over a century over who had the most claim to this feat and finally settled the issue by putting up a plaque in the church honoring them both. Allentown citizens regarded this event as a high point in the city's history, and outdid themselves to give the Liberty Bell a rousing welcome in Allentown as it journeyed back from the Chicago Fair in 1893. The rail car carrying the Liberty Bell was run right down the Hamilton Avenue trolley tracks; five thousand people marched in a parade for the Bell and a memorial service was held in the Zion Reformed Church.

If Allentown had to rely on its contribution to American history, little would have been heard from it again. Fortunately, Allentown enjoyed some more tangible resources: proximity to the Pennsylvania anthracite beds, and a location on both the Lehigh Valley Canal and the Lehigh Valley Railroad, which transported the anthracite to Philadelphia and into a series of canals and railroads which eventually took it to New York. Construction related to both the canal and railroad inadvertently led to the discovery of natural cement deposits along the Lehigh and eventually made the Lehigh Valley one of the cement capitals of the world.

In the first two decades of the nineteenth century, the major obstacle to making money from the anthracite in the Mauch Chunk Hills some twenty miles to the north of Allentown was the problem of transporting it to market down the rapid-plagued Lehigh River. An impoverished Philadelphia nailmaker, Josiah White, devised a crude but ingenious solution to the second problem in 1819. He constructed V-shaped so-called "bear trap gates" over each of the rapids. The gates were filled with water, which was then released in a volume sufficient to carry a coal-bearing "ark" over the dangerous rocks. The "arks," twenty five feet long and sixteen feet wide, were dismantled in Philadelphia. The lumber was sold and the spikes and nails were sent back to Mauch Chunk for reuse. With machine saws to cut the planks, a new ark could be assembled for a downstream journey in forty-five minutes. By 1823 a thousand tons of the "black stones" had glutted the unprepared Philadelphia market and the price was cut in half. In 1829 the Lehigh Canal, a combination of canals and slack water stretches was completed, making two-way water traffic possible.

It was the discovery, along the route of the Lehigh Canal, of a substance called hydraulic limestone that allowed the canal builders to prepare their own water-resistant mortar for the construction of locks and spillways, rather than import the expensive material from Europe. Another big deposit of this limestone was found in the 1850's in the course of blasting deep cuts through the cliffs along the Lehigh River for the Lehigh Valley Railroad.

David Saylor of Allentown and two partners started the first natural cement manufacturing plant in the Lehigh Valley in 1851. Twenty years later, Saylor got the patent for the U.S. manufacture of the more durable portland cement, which required more complete combustion of the limestone at higher temperatures. The Allentown cement industry took off in the eighteen-nineties, when there was a tenfold increase in production, due partly to the lowered cost of the newly introduced rotary kiln method and partly to the greatly increased demand for cement for building with reinforced concrete. By 1908 there were eleven cement mills within a six-mile radius, employing twelve thousand men and producing six million barrels of cement annually, about 40 percent of the total U.S. cement production.

Adequate railroad connections and adequate coal power allowed Allentown to exploit another important resource—the reputation of its work force for skill and reliability. That reputation may have been due in part to Allentown's high percentage of established German families. Owners of silk mills in Paterson, undoubtedly exasperated by the unruly work force there, opened branches in Allentown. One of these, the Phoenix, has gone on to become one of the country's biggest manufacturers of men's wear, currently employing about twelve hundred workers. Allentown's silk industry, however, never got bigger than a tenth of Paterson's, nor did its iron and steel industry get bigger than a fifth of Troy's.

In 1906 Joseph Mack, an Allentown silk businessman, persuaded his brothers Jack and Augustus to move their embryonic bus and truck concern from Brooklyn to Allentown, where land and labor were cheaper. Fearful of losing their big city image, the Mack Brothers somewhat incongruously named their first Allentown-produced truck "the Manhattan," but the shorter, tougher "Mack" name stuck. The big break came during World War I, when Mack sold the U.S. Army several thousand "Bulldog" trucks and got free advertising with thousands of U.S. soldiers. Mack has its corporate headquarters south of the city and now employs six thousand.

In the twentieth century Allentown has continuously attracted big manufacturing companies. The city's population increased from 70,000 to 109,000 between 1920 and 1970, evidence of vitality which sets it apart from most other gritty cities. Allentown has capitalized on its location at the center of a rich manufacturing area to become a major retail center as well, drawing customers from all the smaller cities in the surrounding area.

A tiny, chauvinist pamphlet put out in 1921 by the Allentown Chamber of Commerce quotes this description of Allentown in a contemporary *National Geographic Magazine* article: "Walk from one end of Hamilton Street to the other in the summer-time and every lamp post you see supports a basket of flowers. Think of a bouquet-studded street several miles long. In winter, evergreens take the place of the blossoms in the baskets. The effect is charming. But it is characteristic of Allentown and the Spirit of Pennsylvania."

Flower baskets still hang from the street lamps along Hamilton Avenue and the effect is still charming. Allentown has by far the most attractive retail section of any of the twelve cities in this book. Four long blocks totalling nearly a half mile along Hamilton Avenue have been transformed into Hamilton Mall. The chief effect has been created by a system of curved plexiglass and steel walkways. The transparent glass over the walkways permits a dramatic view from the entire mall of the flag-bearing figure atop the Soldiers and Sailors Monument at Seventh Street and Hamilton Avenue.

Three department stores, Leh's, Zollinger's and the regionally famous Hess's are located within Hamilton Mall, their gracious storefronts set off by the walkways. Parking is ample, provided by the department stores, and one of the earliest downtown Park and Shop programs, formed by the merchants along Hamilton Avenue in 1946.

To the east of Hamilton Mall is a modern civic center constructed in an urban renewal area which has some blank spaces but no gaping holes. The ornate old courthouse next door to its modern replacement remains as the city's Art Museum and Historical Society.

Stretching north, east and west of Hamilton Mall, from about Fifth to Twelfth Streets, are blocks and blocks of cheerful rowhouses in red brick with white trim. There are delightful varieties of gables and turrets and jigsaw trim on porches. But the special ornaments, unique to Allentown, are the many varieties of curved wooden awnings over the doors. A whole block of them gives the effect of an undulating line. Similar but smaller rowhouses, also with wooden awnings and gables, are found across Jordan Creek in an area of old mills.

In all but a very few areas, the residences are in good condition. Citizen neighborhood groups, organized by the Allentown city government, encourage owners to renovate their houses. There is just the beginning of a fashionable movement of families back from the suburbs. The Leh family, owners of Leh's department store, became trend setters when they fixed up two houses for their residence on Walnut Street, a block off Hamilton Avenue. In an area called Old Town, which includes several blocks around Eighth and Chew Streets, young professionals are moving in, and townhouse prices are beginning to go up. Interestingly enough, one of the things the new owners seem to be doing is removing the old awnings that are the special mark of Allentown, all in the name of "restoration" to a colonial look that probably was never there.

In keeping with the pleasant, hometown character of its housing, Allentown has built its further reputation on its parks, bands and huge county fair. Attracting over seven hundred thousand visitors during ten days in August, the Allentown county fair was the biggest in America in 1890 and remains one of the biggest today. Unfortunately, the very ornate gatehouse of the 1890's hasn't survived, but the racetrack and little kiosks are reminders of the fun to be had during fair season.

A cement millionaire, General Henry Clay Trexler, brought experts to Allentown in the 1920's to develop a park plan. The General also gave his own 142 acre estate, now known as Trexler Memorial Park on the West Side of town, as well as a game preserve of over a thousand acres ten miles northeast of town. Closer to downtown, there are several miles of parkway along both Cedar Creek and the Little Lehigh Creek.

The bandstand in West Park off Fifteenth Street is used during the summer by five citywide bands and by the Allentown Symphony for pops concerts. Four of the bands were founded before 1910 and one of them, the Allentown Band (founded in 1828), is the nation's oldest civilian concert band. Allentown likes to call itself "Band City, U.S.A."

In the balance of flavor and pleasure, Allentown is short on the former and long on the latter. Among the gritty cities it stands as the extreme opposite of Paterson, which is long on colorful history and short on contemporary amenities. With its low unemployment and its location in a rich county, Allentown has only to avoid squandering the great advantages it has among gritty cities and latch onto the nationwide back-to-the-city movement. With a little luck it should remain a very livable city indeed.

2. *Hamilton Mall looking west from Sixth Street*

ldiers and Sailors Monu-
Seventh and Hamilton

4. *Shopping on Hamilton Mall*

5. *House at Eighth and Linden Streets,
Hess Co. parking facility behind*

6. Industrial area between Jordan Creek and the Lehigh River

7. Recycled downtown moviehouse, Eighth Street off Hamilton Mall

8. *Industry adjacent to Fountain Park, where Mack stored new trucks for shipment during World War I*

9. *Grandstand at the Fairgrounds, Seventeenth and Chew Streets*

10. *Meatpacking plant near the Lehigh River*

11. *Linden Street turrets*

12. *Gordon Street in the Old Town neighborhood*

13. West End rowhouses

14. *Awnings on Fifth Street*

15. *Tilghman Street rowhouses*

16. *Rowhouses on Sixth Street*

17. *Awnings on Liberty Street near Eighth Street*

BETHLEHEM

BETHLEHEM IS A SCHIZOPHRENIC AT PEACE WITH BOTH OF its selves. The origins of the city's split personality and its peacefulness go back to the very beginning.

In December 1741 a small group of Moravians, members of the missionary sect the House of Brethren, gathered in a log house on the banks of the Monocacy, where the creek flows into the Lehigh, to celebrate Christmas Eve. The singing was led by Count Zinzendorf, the European patron of the sect, who had come to spend a year visiting its North American colonies. Late in the evening he began the hymn "Nicht Jerusalem Sondern Bethlehem" (Not Jerusalem But Bethlehem) and in the minds of the Moravians gathered there to start a communal life of work and worship, the place was henceforth to be Bethlehem.

A little over a hundred years later, in 1845, the Moravian church gave up both its mandate to govern Bethlehem and its claim to exclusive control of land. The church sold off four large farms to the south of the Lehigh River. Shortly afterwards a new town was laid out and a lot was sold off in 1853 to the first industry, the Pennsylvania and Lehigh Zinc Company. In 1855 the Lehigh Valley Railroad, constructed on the south side of the Lehigh River, was opened for passengers between Easton to the east and Allentown to the west. And in 1863 the first blast furnace of the Bethlehem Iron Company began operating.

1. Bethlehem Steel Mills from the playing fields near Nisky Hill Cemetery

Thus South Bethlehem was started as an industrial colony and source of wealth for the Moravians in the orderly town of Bethlehem to the north. The Moravians deliberately fostered this colony as they had fostered the creation of religious colonies before. Since their religion accepted business as a way of participating in life, they invested in the concerns to the south. But because they loved the orderly life of their community in Bethlehem, very few actually went to live in South Bethlehem, and Bethlehem proper remained above all a respectable community.

The efforts of the Moravians in creating and perpetuating a high level of cultural life in Bethlehem to this day are unique among colonization efforts in America. Within a few years after their arrival in 1741, the Moravians constructed several stone communal houses with long sloping roofs and two stories of dormers that have a look quite distinct from any other eighteenth-century American architecture. The Brothers' House and the Sisters' House quartered single men and women. Another building housed married couples, and a fourth, the Widows' House, is still occupied by Moravian widows.

These buildings line Church Street and form a group between the Moravian Church at the corner of Church and Main Streets and the Moravian cemetery, God's Half Acre, along Market Street. They are solid and peaceful buildings. The later colonial houses of stone and brick that line Church Street and Market Street to the east of the Moravian buildings continue the soft colors and sober lines.

From the very beginning the Moravians expressed part of their religious belief through music. They founded the Collegium Musicum in 1744. Travellers from Europe brought the first copies of Haydn's symphonies and quartets to be played in Bethlehem in the late 1780's and 1790's. The orchestra was renamed the Philharmonic Society in the first decade of the nineteenth century and performed the American premiere of the Haydn Creation in 1811. In 1900 the Bach Choir was founded; it has conducted Bach festivals almost every year for decades, attracting concert-goers from the entire region and beyond, especially at Christmas.

The Moravians also organized education for their young from the very beginning. They founded a School for Boys and a School for Girls within the first two years of their arrival, and by the late nineteenth century their Seminary for Young Ladies attracted pupils from thirty-two of the Union's thirty-eight states. The Moravian College and Seminary enrolled less than ten new male students each year to study for six years with a tiny dedicated faculty. Today Moravian College enrolls twelve hundred men and women.

Meanwhile a more rambunctious town was developing on the south side of the Lehigh as workers came to the zinc and iron mills. The first noticeable group was Pennsylvania German, a far less educated and cultured group than the Moravians. They spoke a weird mixture of German and English, as the punch line of a contemporary ad shows: "un bringt eier greenbacks mit. Wholseal for cash—sell is unser style" (reprinted in *Bethlehem: the Golden Years*). Then came the Irish and, beginning in the 1870's, the oppressed minorities of the Austro-Hungarian Empire, Slovaks and, especially, Hungarians.

A little worker housing was built by the iron company, but mostly the workers were on their own for housing throughout the late nineteenth century. In 1870 the *Daily Times* hoped that "capitalists will cast their eyes South-Bethlehem-ward as the demand for houses is steadily on the rise." But in 1893 the paper reported that most of the 168 houses built the previous year were "built by workingmen and others who will personally inhabit them." The existing houses in South Bethlehem reflect this piecemeal construction. Although there are a few places where houses have been built alike and in rows, mostly the houses are scattered up the hillsides, each very different from the next.

South Bethlehem developed its industrial reputation slowly and steadily. The Bethlehem Iron Company started its first blast furnace in 1863. Its major product was steel rails. In 1886, armed with technical knowledge acquired on a visit to big European steel companies, the directors of the Iron Company bid successfully on a contract to make the steel forgings and armor plate for the U.S. Navy. Within thirty months they constructed an enormous steel forging plant for the contract, but they ended up sharing the work with Carnegie's Pittsburgh plant because they could not meet the deadline alone. For years Carnegie and Bethlehem split the armor plate and gun forgings business between them.

The transformation of Bethlehem Iron Company into the Bethlehem Steel Corporation took place in a series of very complicated financial mergers between 1898 and 1904. The result was a company that made steel and built ships under the control of Charles Schwab, who had been president of U.S. Steel before a falling out with its directors. When Schwab took over he launched the company into a massive program of expansion, based in part on a stronger type of structural steel in an "H" form rather than the traditional "I."

Bethlehem Steel increased its production enormously during World War I, doing work for England, China, and other foreign countries. Schwab paid generous dividends out of the profits and had enough money left over to purchase other steel plants all over the East. The company's South Bethlehem work force rose from 9,712 in January 1915 to 21,705 in January 1918. In all the company produced three hundred ships, eighteen million rounds of ammunition, almost four thousand field guns, and thirty-two thousand tons of armor plate.

Beginning as early as the 1880's, deliberate attempts were made to attract industries which would employ women and children. The *Daily Times* reported in 1886 that a delegation to New York City had been successful in persuading a silk mill to relocate in South Bethlehem "to take up the light labor of the town." South Bethlehem was successful in attracting numerous textile mills and cigar factories, many of which are still standing.

Lehigh University was founded as a technical institute after the Civil War by the manager of the Lehigh Valley Railroad, who had been left rich from war profits. The University was so generously endowed that tuition was free for twenty years.

In the early twentieth century the Borough of South Bethlehem was a strange mixture of people. On the one hand there were Central and Southern European ethnic communities with their prominent and varied churches and lavish celebrations of religious holidays. They concentrated along Third Street south to the river and on the southeastern hillsides. On the hillsides to the west (towards Allentown) stood the buildings of the Lehigh campus, the houses of its faculty, and beyond, on Fountain Hill, the lavish houses of the nouveau riche entrepreneurs.

The movement to join far-from-staid South Bethlehem with Bethlehem proper, still dominated by the Moravians, began in the 1890's as South Bethlehem businessmen realized first that municipal services were more costly to provide on a small scale, and second that the small city presented a less attractive setting to new industry than full-scale cities such as nearby Allentown and Easton. At a public meeting in 1904, the Chief Burgess of Bethlehem complained that "people go to Allentown and buy the same thing for the same price they can obtain in Bethlehem because it is simply the idea of going to Allentown." Until the First World War three times as many businesses in Allentown and Easton advertised in the Bethlehem *Globe* as did businesses from Bethlehem. And no wonder, for the only link between the two Bethlehems was an ancient covered bridge infamous for long delays caused by grade crossings in the freight yards on the south side. The two towns were long unable to agree on a plan for a high-level bridge.

Consolidation finally came about in 1917, due partly to the unifying spirit of the war, partly to the good feelings generated by a successful campaign to raise money from both Bethlehems for the Hill-to-Hill bridge, and most of all to the efforts of Charles Schwab and other Bethlehem Steel executives who had supported civic activities on behalf of both Bethlehems and had projected the company's image as a Bethlehem firm.

In present-day Bethlehem, all this history is very evident. The Moravian district stands virtually unchanged. The steel mill towers above activities on both sides of the Lehigh River, glowing by night, by day as grimy as the hundred years of blast furnaces that preceded it. Some of the worker housing in South Bethlehem has been torn down for expansion of the steel plant. Saint Michael's cemetery, where immigrants are buried, is in ruins. Some blocks of housing and commercial buildings along Second Street are deteriorating. But Orthodox, Protestant and Catholic churches line Third Street, clearly visible from the porches and fenced backyards of the neat little houses that look down on them from the hillsides.

The evidence of misguided efforts at renewal is minimal. There are one or two blocks still vacant in South Bethlehem, and a one-block pedestrian mall in Bethlehem has proved hard to rent and an irritant to automobiles; but otherwise, the city's efforts at revitalization are appropriately modest and attractive. The modern civic center overlooks the Lehigh River and the South Bethlehem hillsides. Facades along Main Street have been spruced up into an attractive tourist-oriented shopping area that fits in well with the old Moravian buildings.

But, as appealing as all this is, Bethlehem cannot hope to support its population with Christmas tourists and concert-goers. It is a much bigger, much more complex city than it was when these cultural traditions were started. In ironic contrast to this urbane elegance, the economic prospects of Bethlehem are tied more than those of any other gritty city to the ups and downs of a single heavy industry. The city's long term survival depends on healthy and growing iron and steel production.

2. *Central Moravian Church (1803) and Brethren's House (1748) from the Hotel Bethlehem in the Christmas season (South Bethlehem in background)*

3. Widows' House (1768) in the old Moravian historic district

4. Detail of Sisters' House (1744)

5. *Market Street residences*

6. *Houses on Church Street*

8. The Tannery (1761) in the restored industrial area along the Monocacy

9. Old textile mill along the Lehigh from the Hill-to-Hill Bridge

10. *Trestle across the Lehigh, with Lehigh Valley R.R. office building behind*

11. *Steel mills in South Bethlehem from the Civic Center*

12. *The Bethlehem Steel mills*

13. The Civic Center with South Bethlehem beyond

14. *South Bethlehem neighborhood, East Packer Avenue*

15. Hillside rowhouses, South Bethlehem between Third and Fourth Streets

16. Housing near the steel mills

17. *Donegan School playground, South Bethlehem*

BRIDGEPORT

FOR MOST PEOPLE, BRIDGEPORT IS JUST ONE MORE STRETCH
of the Connecticut Turnpike—from Exits 24 through 30. For
some five miles, the city's factories, neighborhoods and downtown are opened to the impatient glances of speeding motorists.

A better way to see Bridgeport is from Pleasure Beach, a long
spit to the east of the Harbor. From the long piers stretching
back from the beach towards downtown, there is a clear view
of highrises, factories, and two huge power plants, all cut at the
waist by the Turnpike. The city spreads along Long Island
Sound, a series of fragments held together by fifteen bridges
across the Pequonnock River and the mile-long Yellow Mill
Channel.

The town of Bridgeport was born reluctantly in 1821. The
borough of Bridgeport and the village of Stratfield were thrust
out of Stratford township and left with little in the way of resources and only about a thousand feet of seacoast. Furious, the
former citizens of Stratford entered a resolution of protest on
the record of the first Bridgeport town meeting. As reported
in Elsie Danenberg's history of Bridgeport, they formally declared that "by an unconstitutional and unjust act they had
been deprived of their rights as citizens of the town of Stratford" and furthermore "that they had been deprived of their

P. T. Barnum Museum on Main Street

lawful name as a town [Stratford] and 'have another imposed upon them [Bridgeport] all without their consent.' "

Fortunately, Bridgeport had an adequate harbor. The first steamboat run to New York City began in 1824, and by 1846 there were two steamboats a day to New York. The fastest could make the trip in a little over three hours. The harbor was improved in 1871 and again by the federal government in World War I. In 1897 over 18,000 vessels cleared the port. By 1916 this had so increased that over 15,000 cleared the port in the month of March alone. Bridgeport was also connected to other cities by railroad early on: to Connecticut towns to the northwest via the Housatonic Railroad in 1836, to the Waterbury brass industry via the Naugatuck Railroad in 1848 and to New York via the New Haven Railroad in 1849.

Only a few industries got started because of local inventions. Instead, Bridgeport seemed to attract entrepreneurs who had begun elsewhere and wanted to expand their businesses; valves and lace, brake linings and sewing machines, scissors and adding machines were all products with national recognition that were manufactured in Bridgeport.

Some products might have brought great wealth to Bridgeport but didn't. The manufacture of the Locomobile, the gasoline engine version of the Stanley Steamer, was transferred to Bridgeport from Newton, Massachusetts in the first decade of the twentieth century. Unlike Henry Ford, the owners of the Locomobile Company of America decided on a high-priced, low-volume operation, and limited production to four cars a day. As George Waldo, Jr. explained in his 1917 history of Bridgeport, "by concentrating on a few cars, they can be made finer. It is thus possible to give intimate attention to each car and each owner."

The company began to make money during World War I with a Locomobile truck (called the Riker, to distinguish it from that "exceedingly aristocratic vehicle," the Locomobile proper) when the British government placed an order for a thousand. Unlike Mack Trucks of Allentown, which sold trucks to the U.S. Army, Locomobile's sales did not build a market in America. The company did not survive the twenties.

Two other products, guns and corsets, brought the city enviable wealth. Dr. Warner's Health Corset, which boasted shoulder straps to keep it up, was first manufactured in McGrawville, New York, but the firm moved to Bridgeport two years later in 1876. By 1917, the production rate was 120,000 corsets per week, and employment reached 3,000.

Warner's came up with a whole series of innovations; the first corset sold with hose supporters, the first brassiere, the first elasticized corsets, and the first corsets with rustproof bones. Waldo's history of Bridgeport claimed that "there is scarcely a town of any size through all the civilized globe in which Warner's corsets cannot be purchased and in which Warner's advertisements are not seen." In 1900, 22 percent of all corsets sold in the U.S. came from Bridgeport.

Warner's was innovative in employee relations as well. In 1887, it opened the Seaside Institute as a gathering place and educational institution for its female employees. With a library, classrooms, restaurant and parlors, the Institute was one of the first of its kind in the country. The building is still standing, dark and brooding, while possible new uses are discussed.

The old corset factory buildings themselves have found a new life as University Square, a shopping center which combines craft boutiques, a clock shop, a restaurant, and factory outlet stores. So far the enterprise is successful and the Bridgeport savings bank underwriting it is planning an expansion.

Bridgeport got even more out of the arms industry. In 1867 the Remington Arms Company of Ilion, New York, established a Bridgeport branch. In 1912 it merged with Union Metallic Cartridge Company and moved its headquarters to Bridgeport.

During World War I the employment of both companies multiplied. In November 1915 there were three thousand employees at Remington Arms. Within six months there were sixteen thousand; another twenty thousand joined over the following year. As Elsie Nicholas Danenberg wrote: "All day long a line of men stood outside the Remington Arms Company, and it was said of the firm that one new man joined the force every 20 minutes." Union Metallic Cartridge Company went from two thousand to seven thousand men over the same period.

The influx of workers into the arms and other war industries placed a great strain on housing and government services in Bridgeport as the population of the city increased by 45 percent in a period of twenty months after war broke out in 1914. Workers were sleeping in two and three shifts in boarding houses, and new workers became reluctant to come to Bridgeport because of the housing shortage. Remington Arms eventually established a real estate department and constructed over 500 units in four- and six-family housing and fourteen dormitories, each for fifty girls.

In 1916 the Bridgeport Housing Company was formed as a public corporation to tackle the housing shortage with federal government help. It constructed a thousand new housing units in about eight locations. Some of these public housing projects are strikingly attractive; for example, Seaside Village is a group of small brick two-story apartment units set around a park. The World War I public housing was a clear departure from the large wooden houses that had been built for decades.

These plain but comfortable-looking wooden houses still constitute much of the look of Bridgeport. There are blocks and blocks of them to the north and west of downtown all the way out to Black Rock. In large areas of East Bridgeport these houses have a battered look with peeling paint and rickety porches. The city is trying a counterattack with rehabilitation loans in the area around Washington Park. The program is expected to improve about two hundred units in the late nineteen seventies.

To the west of downtown, the houses are by and large kept crisply painted in pastel colors that convey a feeling of being close to the ocean. Around Clinton Avenue, there is a fine set of much larger and fancier Victorian houses that are being used for professional and institutional offices. The area was rezoned in the early seventies in hopes that these new permitted uses would save it from a process of deterioration. It seems to be working.

Bordering the ocean for about three miles to the west of downtown, Seaside Park allows one to be close to the sea yet shaded under broad trees, a combination virtually unique along the ocean front of the northeast coast. There are bouncing horses and swings and a circus-like hotdog stand in warm weather. The trees taper off and disappear along the coast to the west. The beach turns into a rocky spit leading out to a lighthouse.

By the turn of the century, Bridgeport was known as the Park City because it had more parks and more acres in parks than almost any other city of its size. The nucleus of Seaside Park was donated in 1865 by four donors who continued to add to it over the next two decades. Beardsley Park, named after its donor, was given to the city in 1878. Laid out in 1881 by America's premier park planner, Frederick Law Olmstead, it lies along the Pequonnock River to the north of downtown.

In the center of Seaside Park is a statue of P. T. Barnum, his ample form surveying all from a comfortable armchair. It is a tribute to the great showman's gifts of land to Seaside Park; but it is also recognition of his role as the entrepreneurial muse of Bridgeport in the second half of the nineteenth century.

The traces left by P. T. Barnum in Bridgeport's history and landscape are remarkable considering that he didn't come to town until already established in his lengthy career. Once there, he was never around for more than a few months at a time as he pursued money-making endeavors all over the globe.

Barnum found the famous midget Tom Thumb, then a child, in Bridgeport in 1841 and went on to exhibit him throughout Thumb's life. In 1848, he built an incredible residence named Iranistan, a Moorish extravaganza with dozens of onion domes. The building was featured in the nationally circulated illustrated newspapers of the time, but was destroyed by fire ten years later. The legacy remains in the form of Iranistan Avenue, which runs from Seaside Park through the west end, and in the remarkable recurrence of the onion-dome motif in the detail of Victorian houses in Bridgeport.

Barnum and a partner laid out Washington Park and surrounding houselots in East Bridgeport in 1851. He then went bankrupt in an unsuccessful attempt to bring a clock manufacturing enterprise to Bridgeport.

It wasn't until 1870 that he started the Greatest Show on Earth, which eventually established its winter quarters in Bridgeport. He had a brief stint as Mayor of Bridgeport in 1875–1876, during which he was responsible for planting hundreds of trees along Bridgeport's streets. Finally, at the end of his career he established what is now the Barnum Museum in downtown Bridgeport just off the Connecticut Turnpike. Carved to rival the most elaborate Indian temple, the building houses Tom Thumb memorabilia, circus models and a huge mechanical Swiss village. Bridgeport revives Barnum's memory every Fourth of July with a Circus Parade.

The twentieth century has contributed its own small bits of frivolity to Bridgeport's life. The ubiquitous Frisbee got its start in East Bridgeport at the Frisbee Baking Company, where employees used to sail pie plates across the room. The bakery is closed now, but just across the way is an enormous new Jai-Alai court with super-graphics that show there's still some fun left in town.

Otherwise the city comes across as solid, comfortable, and unpretentious. Bridgeport is one of the few gritty cities to have essentially completed an extensive urban renewal of its downtown. In contrast to Lancaster's beautifully designed but economically shaky renewal project, Bridgeport's shopping mall, garage and franchise hotel are unprepossessing in appearance but economically sound. The future seems stable if not brilliant. Still, a city that produced P. T. Barnum and the Frisbee is worth keeping an eye on.

2. P. T. Barnum in Seaside Park

3. Fayerweather Island lighthouse from Barnum Boulevard

4. *Seaview Avenue in the East End from the fishing pier on Pleasure Beach*

5. *Downtown Bridgeport from Pleasure Beach*

6. *Washington Square bandstand*

7. *House in East Bridgeport with "Iranistan" detail*

8. *House in the West End showing Barnum's "Iranistan" influence*

9. Orthodox church on East Main Street, East Bridgeport,
viewed from Orchard Street

10. *West End house, Maplewood and Wood Avenues*

11. *Typical Bridgeport wooden houses, Howard Avenue in the West End*

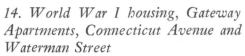

14. *World War I housing, Gateway Apartments, Connecticut Avenue and Waterman Street*

13. *World War I government housing, Bond Street across from the G.E. factory*

16. *Detail of porches, Bond Street houses*

15. *World War I housing, Seaside Village off Iranistan Avenue*

17. *Post Office Arcade, 1001 Main Street*

18. *Refurbished factory, State and Organ Streets*

19. *Peoples Savings Bank Building off McLevy Green*

20. *Lafayette Mall in downtown Bridgeport*

HOBOKEN

HOBOKEN BEGAN AS A PEACEFUL RIVERSIDE RESORT FOR refugees from Manhattan, who wandered along River Walk to the Elysian Fields. Then for some eighty years it became an industrial and waterfront city and acquired a tough reputation. Now, as some industry has moved out and the piers have died, the city is becoming quiet and stable again and is beginning to attract middle class commuters from Manhattan to live in its attractive residential sections. To quote the headline of a 1976 article in the *Washington Post*, "Ho-Ho-Ho Hoboken Has the Last Laugh."

Hoboken is built on one of the very few places along the Jersey shore opposite Manhattan where there is sea-level access to the Hudson River and solid land to build on. At Hoboken the Palisade Cliffs, which line the west bank of the Hudson, move inland just far enough to accommodate an area about twelve by fourteen city blocks.

Into this small area is packed forty-five thousand people. The population per square mile is over thirty-two thousand, higher than that of New York City. At its most crowded, in 1910, the city housed over seventy thousand people, as well as manufacturing firms employing ten thousand workers.

1. Apartment building near Tenth Street and Park Avenue

More than any other gritty city, Hoboken was developed by one man and his family. A remarkable inventor/entrepreneur, Colonel John Stevens, purchased the island (separated from land by marshes on the west) in 1784 for about $90,000, and named it Hoboken from an amalgam of the Dutch and Indian words for it.

At first Colonel Stevens developed Hoboken as a resort, beginning with the six mile path known as the River Walk, later adding a mineral water spa called Cybil's Cave, a tavern, hotel, and a hundred foot high proto-Ferris wheel called the Observation Tower. The first regular organized American baseball game was played in the Elysian Fields in 1846, and the first American yacht club was built in 1844. The place must have offered powerful attractions, because Hoboken can boast large numbers of rich and famous people as early samplers of its pleasures. Alexander Hamilton, Aaron Burr, Lillian Russell, Jay Gould, William Vanderbilt, Horace Greeley and Henry Ward Beecher are all said to have frequented Hoboken's meeting places.

Partly to add convenience and flavor to his real estate, Colonel Stevens invented things. In 1804 the first successful steamboat driven by turn screws, the *Little Juliana*, went into service between Hoboken and the Battery. Despite this success, Colonel Stevens then had to invent a horse-driven paddle wheel boat to carry passengers back and forth until 1824, when he won a long legal battle to break Robert Fulton's steamboat monopoly in the Hudson. In 1825 Stevens designed and built the first experimental steam-driven locomotive in America, which he ran on a circular track in front of one of his Hoboken Inns.

After Colonel Stevens' death in 1838, control of Hoboken passed to his family. Although incorporated as a city in 1855, Hoboken's land was held by the Stevens family through the Hoboken Land and Improvement Company, known as "The Company." Gradually the company began to sell off property for industry and residences while retaining the highest land, Castle Point, for the family.

Stevens Institute of Technology, the oldest college of mechanical engineering in the country, was founded in 1870 with a land grant and endowment from Edwin Stevens. The land to the north and east of Stevens Institute, where the Elysian Fields had been, attracted upper-income buyers. The income level of residents dropped with the elevation to the south and west. In the lowest swampy areas to the west, which flooded in heavy rains until well into the twentieth century, factories were built and surrounded by worker housing. The area southwest of Adams and 4th Streets is the only section of wooden tenements in Hoboken; it was here that Frank Sinatra, Hoboken's best-known son, grew up.

By 1889 there were still only slightly more than three thousand manufacturing workers employed in Hoboken, but by 1909 the number had tripled. Shipbuilding was the primary industry; foundry products and specialized precision instruments were also important. In the late nineteenth century Hoboken began to attract large numbers of immigrants. In 1890, 40 percent of the population was foreign born and well over half of that was German. Until the first World War, Hoboken seemed like a piece of Germany; Germans were the merchants and hotel owners.

At the same time Hoboken was becoming important as a transportation center. The Delaware Lackawanna and Western railroad terminated in Hoboken and commuters from New Jersey to Manhattan used the Hoboken Lackawanna ferries, which remained in service until the sixties. The PATH (Port Authority Trans-Hudson) Tube was finally opened in 1908 after thirty years under construction. Major European steamship lines, such as Hamburg-American, Holland-American and Scandinavian, began to use Hoboken's piers and turned Hoboken into a major trans-Atlantic port. Bars and restaurants flourished from the waterfront business. Two of these, Duke's House and the Clam Broth House, are still attractions.

The First World War began the time of troubles. From 1914 to 1917 seventeen German ships were immobilized at Hoboken piers under harbor neutrality acts. When the U.S. entered the war in 1917, the U.S. government seized the piers, eliminating hundreds of thousands of dollars in tax revenues, for which the city finally received token compensation in 1950. Further revenues were lost from liquor licenses when the government closed bars within a half mile as part of the establishment of a port of embarkation for troops to Europe. Worst of all, the prosperous German community was destroyed. Part of the city was under martial law and Germans were sent to Ellis Island. Thousands of Germans left Hoboken.

By 1920 Italians outnumbered Germans among the foreign born and Hoboken was becoming known as an Italian City. Manufacturing, shipbuilding and the docks remained important. Increasingly, however, the waterfront was plagued with crime and racketeering.

Apart from the soldiers, who knew Hoboken in both World Wars, the American public got its strongest impression of the city from Elia Kazan's 1954 movie *On The Waterfront*. The script, written by Arthur Miller, was based on a 1948 *New York Sun* series of articles by Malcolm Johnson about waterfront corruption. The film is the story of the uncovering of a waterfront crime, and used actual dockworkers as extras. Kazan hired bodyguards to protect him throughout the filming on location in Hoboken. Some $30,000 had to be added to the budget to cover rake-offs and payments to Hoboken landlords charging exorbitant rents. Terry, the character played by Marlon Brando, was based on an actual labor union informant named Arthur J. Browne.

Today the waterfront is nearly dead except for a Bethlehem Steel Shipbuilding yard at the north end of the city. The enormous port authority piers have been closed since 1975, and those just to the north of them have been torn down. Hoboken has lost out to more efficient piers, including containerized facilities such as the banana pier in neighboring Weehawken, and the piers in Port Elizabeth.

However, Hoboken is in the midst of a comeback based on the good condition of its solid housing stock. Hoboken's housing is extraordinarily consistent from one end of the city to the other. There are essentially two types, a relatively small number of three and four story townhouses, and a large number of five story brick and stone walkup apartment buildings. The larger buildings give an impressive canyon effect with their uniform cornice heights on both sides of the street. The buildings have long front steps that boast one of Hoboken's delightful specialties: ornamental iron balustrades, which on a sunny day can give an effect of shimmering black lace. A companion specialty is the lacy iron fire escapes that adorn the taller Hoboken buildings.

Although there has been some urban renewal demolition along River Street near the waterfront, Hoboken officials claim to have resisted this approach and emphasized renovation of housing far more than other cities. One building successfully saved from demolition was the abandoned factory of Keuffel and Esser, a prestigious German manufacturer of drafting tools. In 1976 this building became the Clock Tower Apartments and began renting its 173 large apartments with twelve-foot ceilings. One of the earliest and most dramatic of all factory recycling projects, it has been emulated by other cities.

A consortium, Applied Housing Associates, has renovated three other large apartment buildings under a city-sponsored program using the federal government's subsidy programs for moderate income housing. Several other large apartment buildings, including another factory, are being renovated by other firms. Altogether about a thousand apartment units had been rehabilitated by the end of 1976.

Hoboken's program of subsidized rehabilitation loans to homeowners is by far the biggest program of its kind in any of the gritty cities. The Home Improvement Project uses federal grants-in-aid to provide interest reduction grants to homeowners who have obtained conventional financing and completed their work. The cash grant is adjusted to combine with the bank loan so that the effective interest rate is 3 percent. Combined with apartment rehabilitation, at current rates over a third of the housing units in Hoboken will have been renovated by 1980. Housing values are increasing, especially in the section of attractive brownstone townhouses along Bloomfield Avenue and Garden Street. Some are being bought by white collar commuters to Manhattan.

No Georgetown chicness has yet attached to Hoboken's commerce; the stores along Washington Street and on cross streets remain lively but unpretentious. Many display signs in Italian, and even more in Spanish for the benefit of Hoboken's newest wave of immigrants, which now makes up 45 percent of the population.

But smart shops may yet come to Hoboken, especially if the city's most ambitious redevelopment ploy is successful. The city plans to convert the magnificent Erie Lackawanna terminal down on the waterfront into an arcade of shops and restaurants. The 1907 building is adorned with ornate copper which makes it dazzling even in its present state of neglect. The first stage, slated to begin in early 1978, will make the structure safe and energy-efficient. If all goes well, the architects who designed San Francisco's Ghirardelli Square will then transform the terminal into Hoboken's shopping magnet. Add to this the view of the Manhattan skyline, and little old Ho-Ho-Hoboken might have the last laugh even on San Francisco.

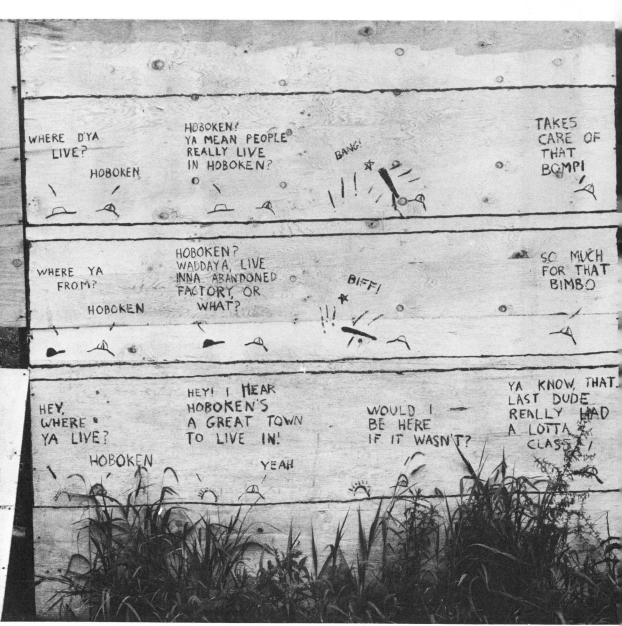

2. *Fence around a construction site, First and River Streets*

3. View from the ruins of Hoboken's piers

4. The old ferry terminal

5. A famous eatery near the terminal

6. *Brownstones on Bloomfield Street*

7. *Fire escape, Hudson and Newark Streets*

8. Balustrades along Park Avenue

9. Apartment houses on Washington Street near Twelfth

11. *Rear yards of the same set of walkups*

. Five-story walkups on Bloomfield Street between Observer Highway
d Newark Street

12. *Clock Towers, Third Street between Adams and Jefferson, an early adaptive use project which converted an old precision instruments factory into apartments*

13. *Waterside warehouse from Thirteenth and Washington Streets*

14. *View from Twelfth Street and Willow Avenue with rehabilitation underway*

15. A shop on Washington Street

16. Columbus Park on Columbus Day, 1977

LANCASTER

1. Story-and-a-half house on Water Street near Orange

THE STONE HITCHING POSTS THAT LINE THE ALLEYS
around the Central Market in downtown Lancaster are well-
kept and well-used. The Amish farmers who come to town tie
their buggies there and go about their business, often at the
same stalls and stores their ancestors visited. Half of the farmers
in Lancaster County are Amish or Mennonites; the soil and the
farming practices they inherited combine to make the value of
their agricultural products greater than that of any other non-
irrigated county in the United States. There is a reflection of
this solidity and sobriety in the look of the City of Lancaster.

Despite nineteenth-century industrialization, twentieth-century suburbanization, and the gross commercialization of the
Amish culture that assaults the eye with endless miles of mo-
tels, restaurants, and wax museums along Route 30 east of town,
the city itself has never lost its sense of purpose—to serve as
the market for the surrounding agricultural community. Lancaster today is streets of neat colonial homes, well cared-for
shops, and tasteful public buildings that look like they are there
first and foremost to serve those who have to go to town for
something.

One of the first inland cities in America, Lancaster was also
the largest such city in the colonial era. The road to Philadelphia

was the first turnpike and the first surfaced highway in America. Later the road served as the main link between Philadelphia and an extensive system of canals built by the Commonwealth of Pennsylvania to win back trade lost to New York on the Erie Canal's success. The Main Line Canal ran from Columbia, west of Lancaster, for 606 miles over the Alleghenies to Pittsburgh, the longest and costliest undertaking of its kind in America. When the railroads followed in the mid-nineteenth century, they passed to the north of Lancaster, causing the city to turn its attention back to its role as regional marketplace.

When industry came to Lancaster, it was tied closely to the agriculture of the area. The three most important products were tobacco (especially cigars), textiles, and livestock. By 1890 there were 8,200 manufacturing jobs in Lancaster, over one quarter of them in the tobacco industry. Most of the operations were small scale; there were 126 tobacco warehouses within the city limits at that time, and 750 in the county. Many of the tobacco warehouses and associated factories are still standing in parts of Lancaster, in some cases renovated and adapted to new uses.

The textile industry employed twelve hundred by 1890 and centered around the Conestoga mills, named after the same stream as the local wagon that opened the West. The stock-yards remained important long after these other industries began to wane.

As it grew as a commercial center, Lancaster began to attract a wide array of merchants. Some families stayed for generations in the same business; the city boasts the oldest hardware firm in the nation, the oldest tobacco shop, and, until its recent closing, the oldest department store operated continuously on the same site by the same family. Other merchants went on to bigger things. One was Milton S. Hershey, who began his chocolate business in Lancaster and lived in a big mansion off the central Penn Square; he later moved his growing business to the nearby town that bears his name. Another was Frank W. Woolworth, who followed a disastrous first attempt at merchandising in upstate New York with a successful store in Lancaster that became the first local "5 and 10." He built what was then Lancaster's tallest building, topped off with an elegant roof garden restaurant.

Lancaster also gave the nation a pair of the least loved political figures of the mid-nineteenth century: James Buchanan, who helplessly presided over the dissolution of the Union before Abraham Lincoln took office; and Thaddeus Stevens, perhaps the most rabid of the Reconstructionists, who capped his career with the successful proposal to impeach President Johnson.

Buchanan remains the only President from Pennsylvania and the only bachelor President. He also served as Minister to Russia under Jackson and as Secretary of State under Polk. He started his law practice in Lancaster in 1812, and wrote soon thereafter with notable candor, "My practice in Lancaster, and some of the adjoining counties, is extensive, laborious, and lucrative." After his term as President he settled back in at Wheatland, an estate on the western outskirts of Lancaster, which he had bought in 1849.

One man to whom Buchanan spoke little in later years was Thaddeus Stevens. As the two rose to national prominence their political differences became ever greater, and remarkably enough, these two Lancaster lawyers became the national leaders of the two major political viewpoints at the most critical time in our history. The Democrat Buchanan opposed slavery but felt the Constitution prevented doing anything about it. Stevens, the Republican abolitionist, sought an end to slavery and punishment for the wicked who had enslaved. Both men died in 1868, Stevens a month after seeing the House of Representatives pass his motion to impeach President Johnson. Both men are buried in Lancaster, with Stevens carrying the battle to his grave in Shreiner's Cemetery, the only one then open to people of all races. His massive stone, inscribed with righteous quotations, stands above the humble markers and crosses that surround it; but no one ever expected humility from Thaddeus Stevens.

Today many streets and neighborhoods of Lancaster look little different than they must have in the nineteenth century and earlier. There is a definite colonial feel without any of the cute or reconstructed look that Americans are accustomed to seeing in such places. Lancaster is not a reconstruction; its homes and shops have been in constant use and have remained because there was no reason to tear them down. By now, of course, there is a great deal of interest in preserving the character and architecture of the city; but it is not the frenetic sort of historic preservation that is evident in other cities, focussing only on a building here or there or an occasional threatened historic site. It is rather a recognition that change is an inevitable economic reality, but that much change can be accommodated without tearing down the things that make the city what it is. Thus there are officially designated historic districts in Lancaster, but they are active neighborhoods with stores and families, not an embalmed block or two. Even careful observers can't really tell when they leave an historic district, because there is care and concern for the past throughout the city.

Two other touches make Lancaster an especially pleasant residential city. One is the use of grids placed on diagonals with each other. The downtown grid runs true north and south, east and west. But within a few blocks one encounters new grids set on diagonals and creating an array of angled streets and intersecting rows of colonial houses. The result is constant variety without the confusion of random pattern. The other delight is in the street names. One set includes King, Queen, Prince and Duke; another is made of Orange, Lemon, Lime, Cherry, Plum and Strawberry.

All this adds to the nursery rhyme look of the occasional little story-and-a-half houses tucked between bigger colonial homes in the older streets of the city. In addition to the historic districts that fill many blocks to the east and northwest of downtown, well-preserved neighborhoods can be found in the West End beginning at Water Street, in the Cabbage Hill area to the southwest off Strawberry Street, and in Hickory Town, to the southeast. Local traditions of building craftsmanship have helped accomplish the extensive rehabilitation being done in these areas; so have loans from the city.

One of the most interesting areas is Hickory Town, now part of an historic district. It was originally slated for the same kind of urban renewal treatment that had demolished blocks of allegedly substandard homes in the adjacent area, only to replace them with tasteless high-rises and vast empty spaces. Lancaster saw early the error in this and, unlike many other cities, had the self-assurance needed to bring it to a halt. The city was helped by the fact that Hickory Town has some of the oldest houses in the city and was the site of the original settlement. It was also helped by a visionary builder who was tired of suburban subdivisions and wanted a new challenge. The result is an exciting and innovative restoration that has retained the traditional colonial streets and converted the rear yards into common open space for the community of houses. A similar effort is about to get underway in an old urban renewal area called the Triangle, across Church Street from Hickory Town. Work there has already uncovered early colonial stone walls under layers of siding. Meanwhile, the mayor has established a policy that no building in the city is to be demolished without his personal approval.

This spirit of revitalization has also begun to be felt in the downtown commercial area, hard hit by a physically attractive but economically unsuccessful urban renewal effort (described in greater detail in the introductory chapter), and by the opening up of a suburban shopping mall with more stores than all of downtown. So far, the new commercial architecture downtown fits in rather well with the old. Recently, the city has begun to interest merchants in making use of the nineteenth- and early twentieth-century facades and other parts of their buildings, by removing the "improvements" of subsequent years that have obscured them.

All this reflects a new set of apparently realistic and achievable goals for downtown Lancaster. The city has decided that the future of its downtown does not lie in fighting the surrounding shopping centers for the average shopper's business; the central business district is too disadvantaged in terms of access, parking, and congestion to make that a battle on good terms. Instead, the city sees downtown as a shopping and service center for a number of specialized groups who can be encouraged—office workers, such as those that Armstrong Cork moved into the urban renewal tower; visitors to the farmers' markets and other historic attractions; and the growing numbers who are choosing to live in the old neighborhoods surrounding downtown.

It seems like a winning combination for Lancaster. And its careful formulation is typical of the way this self-assured city has tried ideas, seen how they worked, and been willing to reject or modify them. There is a greater confidence about the future in Lancaster than in any of the other gritty cities, and it derives from this willingness to try things and make them fit what is special to the city. If the U.S. Conference of Mayors wants to learn what kind of a spirit can save the cities, it should resist the lure of the Astrodome or the Big Apple, and hold its next convention in Lancaster.

2. Stairway on Queen Street, downtown urban renewal area

3. *New hotel and still-vacant shopping arcade, downtown urban renewal area*

4. Shops on Marion Place, downtown

5. The old and new County Courthouses on Duke Street

6. *New and old commercial mix on King Street*

7. *Woodward Street, southeast Lancaster*

8. Corner of Chestnut and Lime Streets

9. Shippen Street homes in the downtown historic district

10. *Part of the stockyards on Marshall Avenue*

11. *Former tobacco warehouse, Plum Street*

12. *One of the Conestoga Mills, South Prince Street*

NORWICH

NORWICH, LIKE READING, IS A CITY BUILT ON HILLS; BUT
instead of railroad yards and locomotive repair shops, its valleys
are filled with fast-flowing streams and falls that empty into the
Thames estuary where downtown stands today. The city is
very old; the earliest settlement dates from 1659. The old village green remains in the Norwichtown sector, surrounded by
streets of fine colonial homes. This section of Norwich resem-
bles a great many other New England towns.

The potential of the Thames for shipping and of the other
streams for mills proved too valuable to allow the place to long
remain a colonial village up in the hills. As early as 1700 the
town appointed a commission to lay out the "east sheep walk,"
which became the access to the landing. Soon after shipbuilding
began and before long a whole new downtown sprang up along
the waterfront.

The city prospered on shipping and shipbuilding until the
blockade during the War of 1812; that experience persuaded
the city to use the mill streams to build a more stable economy.
Between 1813 and 1816 four cotton mills, two woolen mills,
and a nail factory were built at the falls of the Yantic and along
the Shetucket.

But the turn away from shipping was not to last long. The
first steamboat arrived in Norwich in 1816 and regular service

Italianate house on Broad Street

along the coast began the next year. In 1835, a number of Norwich businessmen, impressed with the potential of a combined rail and steamboat service for passengers and freight between Boston and New York via Norwich, formed a company to build the Norwich and Worcester Railroad. The railroad opened in 1840 and met the new line from Boston to Worcester. At Norwich, connections were made with luxurious steamboats that provided predominantly overnight trips to New York. As Farnham carefully details in *The Quickest Route*, the line through Norwich provided a fast, inexpensive, and extremely popular way to travel between the two cities for nearly three quarters of a century. Even after more railroads were built it was still fashionable to take the steamers through Norwich.

Besides the prosperity the steamers brought to the city, they also exposed Norwich to people and events it would otherwise never have experienced. Cornelius Vanderbilt, an early owner of the Norwich and New York Steamboat Company, made his brother captain of one of the craft. Vanderbilt cut his teeth on the steamboat business and used the experience in building his railroad empire. One "steamboat war" he fought in 1844 is described by Farnham. A competitor on the Hudson decided to put a boat on the New York to Providence run; in retaliation Vanderbilt sent boats, including the fast and luxurious *City of Worcester* from the Norwich line, into the Hudson to cut into the invader's business. This caused a local newspaper to "beseech Captain Vanderbilt to make short work of the enemy and bring him to terms as soon as possible, for we can ill afford to spare him and his queenly craft from this, his proper line of duty." Two days later the interloper withdrew to the Hudson, and everything returned to normal.

The state of the shipbuilding art in the latter part of the nineteenth century allowed the launching of a series of incredibly luxurious and profitable steamships for the Norwich line. The *Atlantic* was said to earn one thousand dollars profit per night. In 1881 the line took delivery of the new *City of Worcester*, built by Harlan and Hollingsworth in Wilmington, a company which also specialized in private railroad cars. This ship was called the most elegant on Long Island Sound, and, among other honors, it was awarded the prize for the most musical whistle in New York harbor. The *City of Lowell* went into service in 1894 after going to New York to have its carpets installed by W & J Sloan and its draperies by Arnold Constable. The steamer was a tough as it was sumptuous; it set the record between New York and New London at five hours and thirty-five minutes, and survived to serve in World War II.

Downtown Norwich grew up to cater both to the activity along the Thames and the expanding industries along the other rivers. By the time the elaborate new town hall was completed in 1873 (at the then-exorbitant cost of $350,000), the city was a major transportation hub, as well as a manufacturing center for textiles, paper, nails, stoves, and firearms. To this day, the affluence and exuberance of that era is reflected in the ornate stonework of the business district's buildings. Unfortunately, the old waterfront and railroad terminals have fallen victim to floods, storms, other acts of God, and urban renewal. The last has resulted in the usual mindless demolition and clearance without real prospects for redevelopment. So the city that owes so much to the way it grew down to the water from up above is now left with very little on its waterfront at all.

Rising above downtown and the mills of the river valleys are Norwich's neighborhoods, comprised of prosperous-looking clapboard houses with pleasant gardens and ornate Victorian porches and trim. Oliver Wendell Holmes, in one of his less judicious opinions, described Norwich as "a town of supreme, audacious, Alpine loveliness." The hills are hardly Alpine, but the houses, yards and public gardens might justify the title of L. W. Bacon's 1896 book *Norwich: the Rose of New England.* To this day, a rose festival is held each June.

The houses along Broadway and Washington Avenue and side streets between downtown and Norwich Academy present a three-dimensional catalog of every fashionable nineteenth-century style—Gothic Revival, Italianate, Stick, Queen Anne, and Shingle. Nearly all are in excellent condition despite what must be very high upkeep costs for their ornate details. This is all the more impressive considering that most of the area is essentially unprotected by law from intrusions or demolition. There are two small historic districts in Norwich, one which covers the early nineteenth-century buildings around the park near the Catholic Cathedral, and the other which protects the area surrounding the common in eighteenth-century Norwichtown. One would think that the quality and detail of the later Victorian houses might arouse some interest in their preservation, over a century after some of them were built.

It was along Broadway and nearby streets that Norwich's wealthiest families lived during its heyday of commerce and industry. The ladies and gentlemen of the day gathered on the front lawns and curved porches as they set off on excursions. One of the greatest of these outings was the annual Ivy League regatta on the Thames between Norwich and New London, culminating in the face-off of the Harvard and Yale varsity crews. A contemporary description of the event is provided in Beckford's 1890 publication, *The Leading Businessmen of Norwich and Vicinity*:

> *Early in the day the river begins to swarm with gaily-decked craft, both small and large. Yachts with great streamers of blue or crimson bunting and sheets strung with national flags, decks lined with enthusiastic and exuberant partisans take up their place along the sides of the course, on the east part above the finish. . . . The scenes on shore are none the less marked. Above the finish line, on Winthrop Neck, is an immense grand stand, crowded with onlookers. The shores for long distances are also lined, and the long observation train of twenty-five or thirty cars filled to the brim, flying great banks of red and blue, and sending forth stunning peals of "Rah! Rah! Rah! Yale" "Rah! Rah! Rah! Harvard," draws its winding length slowly up opposite the starting line. Now for a moment there*

*is breathlessness, then the pistol flashes, the stern-
lines from the two boats are dropped by their hold-
ers, and off neck and neck go the two great sweep-
ing lines of oars, followed at a regular distance on
the river by a great and imposing line of steamboats
and smaller craft, on the shore by the observation-
train which now sends forth the sharp staccato Yale
shout, or the longer, deeper Harvard cry, as the
partisans of either side fancy they see their own
colors to the fore. So for four miles straight away
dash the two crews, followed with unbending gaze
by some twenty thousand eyes, and unwearying
exclamations from some ten thousand throats. In
little more than twenty minutes, that seem as many
days to the crews with every muscle strained to its
utmost, and hardly more seconds to the vast watch-
ing concourse, and either the blue or the crimson
has crossed the line, while cannons thunder from
neighboring yachts, and the great annual conflict
on which were settled so many ardent hopes, and
not a few treasured and anxious dollars, is decided.*

Bacon's description of Norwich at the end of the nineteenth century remains apt: "Happily for the beauty of Norwich, the diverse and numerous factories have for the most part disposed themselves along the streams in suburban villages or on side streets, without interfering with the sumptuous residence streets of the city or with the quaint and archaic beauty of the old town. This is not to be taken as implying that there is no beauty in the factory. The magnificent properties of the Ponemah Mill at Taftville have a grace and dignity equal in their way to those of a cathedral."

Taftville, a small community northeast of the main part of town, is still a very impressive part of Norwich. There, along the Shetucket, John F. Slater built the still-renowned Ponemah Mill. The first building, completed in 1873, accommodated fifteen hundred looms to produce the finest fabrics. Reminiscent of a castle along the Rhine, the complex of buildings is still used for manufacturing.

Back from the river and the mills is the town of Taftville with two large mansard-roofed commercial buildings and several blocks of company houses—duplexes and multi-family clapboard structures that are an architectural experience in their own right, as they afford glimpses here and there of the mill towers. Rising up the hillsides behind these are rows of large wooden houses with multiple porches that look out over the town, the mills, and the river.

The charm of Norwich, in short, derives from its having set off to one side its quaint New England origins, and plunged into the business of the nineteenth century. A few pages from Norwichtown in picture-books of old New England homes may occupy the preservationists, but those who look at Norwich as a city are drawn by the richness of that nineteenth-century legacy.

2. *Detail from Italianate house on Broad Street*

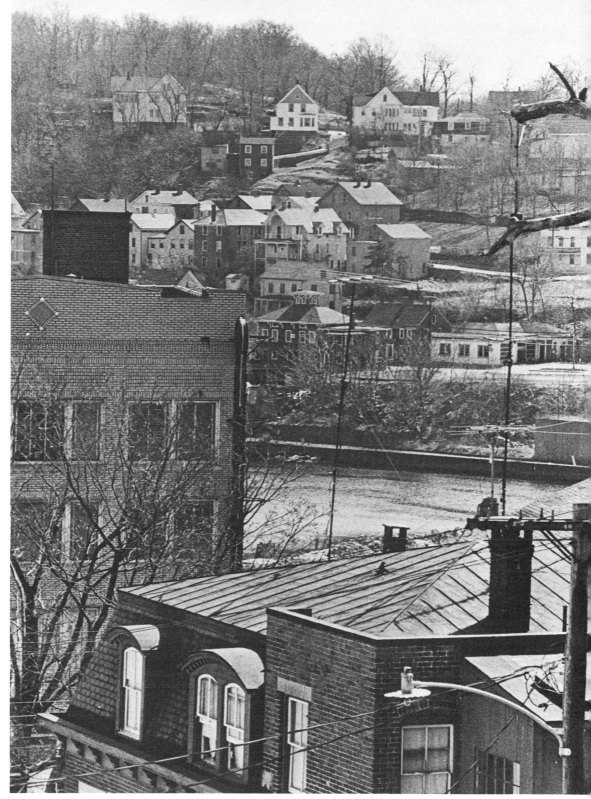

3. *View of Mount Pleasant across the Thames River from Jail Hill*

4. Downtown Norwich

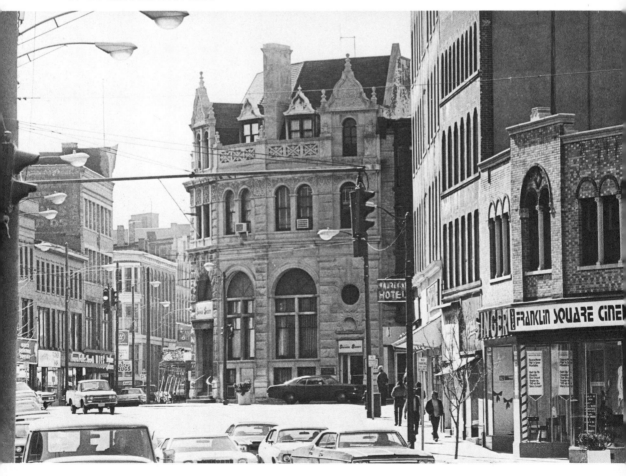

5. *Town Hall*

7. *Cliff Street houses*

6. *Merchants Avenue in Taftville*

8. *Houses above Boswell Avenue*

9. *Detail, house on Broadway*

10. *Detail, house on Williams Street*

11. *One of the houses along Broadway*

12. *Detail, house on Williams Street*

13. *Broad Street near Boswell Avenue*

14. *Worker housing in Taftville*

16. *Detail, Ponemah Mills*

Ponemah Mills on the Shetucket at Taftville

18. *Empty mill below the falls*

Falls of the Yantic, site of earliest industry in Norwich

PATERSON

THERE ARE NO CLASSY RESTAURANTS IN PATERSON. FOR
an interesting evening a good bet is the Question Mark Bar
on Van Houten Street. Tommy, the owner, was a small child
when the bar, run by his parents, became the headquarters for
Elizabeth Gurley Flynn and the other leaders of the Industrial
Workers of the World (the Wobblies), during the great silk
strike of 1913. It was here that the left-wing labor movement
in America reached its peak. Across Van Houten Street from
the bar line up eight of the thirty-odd mill buildings crowded
along the Passaic River a few blocks from the Paterson City
Hall. The streets are dark, and the great falls of the Passaic
thunder a few hundred feet away. The impression is overwhelming: Paterson is a powerful rough town.

There are no classy hotels in Paterson, either. The rag-tag
downtown competitor to the motel franchises in the next town
to the east along the freeway bears the name of Paterson's spiritual and material father, Alexander Hamilton. Paterson was the
site which he chose for the first government-sponsored effort to
create indigenous American industry independent of England.
Hamilton had visited the great falls of Passaic while an officer
in the Revolution and envisioned the falls as the source of power
for this first planned industrial complex in America. The bill he

. Mills below the Great Falls of the Passaic

sponsored to have the U.S. government set up a "national manu-factory" failed to pass Congress, but he found a way to do it privately.

In 1791, with $600,000 in capital, the Society for Establishing Useful Manufactures (S.U.M.) was chartered by the State of New Jersey. The Society, with the continuing advice of Hamil-ton, hired Pierre L'Enfant to design the series of raceways and canals that would distribute power to the mills. L'Enfant's plan, however, proved too much for the Society's limited resources, so they fired him and developed their own system over several decades as income permitted. Three tiers of raceways, each with a head race and a tail race, remain nearly intact today. When kept clear of debris, they add a romantic charm to the rough mills they flow by.

The impressive industrial complex envisioned by Hamilton did not really emerge until the mid-nineteenth century with two major industries, silk and locomotives. Silk grew slowly out of an earlier cotton textile industry. In the 1860's, however, it got a big push from the nearly simultaneous imposition of an Amer-ican protective tariff on foreign silk goods and the removal of an English tariff on French silk goods. From one year to the next, English silk workers in Macclesfield, the broad silk center, and Coventry, the ribbon center, became unemployed. Then, in an extraordinary transfer of skills across the Atlantic, thousands emigrated to Paterson. Emigration societies were formed, and those selected to come to America were honored and sent off by crowds of fellow workers.

Once in Paterson, the transplanted silk workers set up their own handlooms in an area known as Weavertown along 12th Street, and a thousand entered the silk factories. Also influential was the emigration of a small number of men who became the entrepreneurs of Paterson's silk industry. Two of the owners of the biggest silk enterprises, William Ryle and Catholina Lam-bert, began working in the silk industry themselves while chil-dren in England.

The other major industry, locomotives, grew less dramatically. Thomas Rogers, a carpenter and machinery manufacturer, began by examining an English locomotive shipped in parts from England. Two years later, in 1837, he had built his own, the Sandusky. By 1854, 102 engines were built in a year at the Rogers works. Rogers gradually captured a large share of the developing market for locomotives by continuing improvements in the design, including the idea of counterbalancing (weighting the wheel heavier opposite the point where it is connected to the crankshaft and piston). In 1860, two thousand workers were employed in making locomotives. The only other important industries in Paterson were textile machinery, jute and textile dying.

Throughout the remainder of the nineteenth and into the early twentieth century, Paterson grew very fast—from about twenty thousand in 1860 to one hundred thirty-five thousand in 1920. The city had an extraordinarily high rate of immigration. In 1890 the proportion of foreign-born was over 40 percent, largely from England and Ireland. By 1920 the proportion was still 33 percent, a very heterogeneous group of immigrants who now included large groups of Italians and Poles. Men still gather, speaking only Italian, in several coffee houses right down the street from the Question Mark Bar.

As they did nearly everywhere, the Irish immigrants fairly quickly took over politics and ran city hall and the police department, leaving left-wing politics to the Italian and Slavic immigrants. In the early twentieth century, Paterson had a reputation as a hotbed of anarchism, producing the anarchist assassin of King Umberto I of Italy, an anarchist newspaper, and at least one anarchist strike.

The Great Silk Strike began in January of 1913 as a dispute over a speed-up in piece work requirements. Within a month after the Wobblies arrived, twenty-five thousand workers and three hundred factories were idle. Hundreds of strikers were arrested and children of strikers were evacuated to stay with sympathizing families outside Paterson. There was a dramatic funeral for two Italian workers that had been killed.

After several months, some workers were ready to negotiate shop by shop, but the Wobblies insisted on a universal agree-

ment for an eight hour day and twelve dollars per week minimum pay. To dramatize the plight of the workers, they staged
a pageant of the Paterson strike in Madison Square Garden
before an audience of fifteen thousand, using over one thousand
strikers and their families in the production. They provided
every detail, including the clatter of the looms, the pathos of
the funeral march for the dead workers, and the violent clashes
with the police.

In the end, however, the workers did negotiate shop by shop
and made no gains in work conditions. There were no perma-
nent shop unions and the silk industry soon entered a long period
of decline as rayon and other synthetics were developed.

There is virtually no company housing in Paterson and very
few signs of development housing. Generally the houses are one
of a kind detached houses of all sizes and shapes, set very close
together. One of the few identifiable residential neighborhoods is
Dublin, an area to the south of the historic mill district. It was
settled by Irish immigrants from 1850 to 1870. The houses are
plain wood, in good condition, and painted light colors; but the
overall effect is something of a jumble.

It is not by mere chance that the mill buildings are still standing in Paterson. In 1967, John Young, a Columbia student of
architecture, and Mary Ellen Kramer, the Mayor's wife, organized a movement to save the old mill section from destruction
by a proposal to extend Route 20 right through them. The highway was stopped, and by 1970 the great falls were declared a
National Natural Landmark. In 1971, 89 acres of the mill district (later expanded to 119 acres) were declared a National
Historic District. While the New Jersey Department of Transportation still owns a number of mills that are woefully neglected, the city feels confident that the future of the district
lies in its restoration and reuse.

Paterson is today the scene of intensive study of its industrial
past through the techniques of industrial archaeology. There are
efforts underway to preserve some of the most important old
mill buildings by finding new uses for them. Industrial archaeol-
ogists in 1974 and 1975 dug and analyzed the remains of several

locomotive works that lay in the path of a storm sewer, linked to nearby construction of Interstate 80. They also prepared essays on industrial history for a symposium held in Paterson in 1974. Their findings lent impetus to efforts by the Great Falls Development Corporation to find funds for reusing the old buildings. Comprehensive Employment Training Act (CETA) funds were used to renovate a mill building, one floor of which is now used for a church-sponsored elementary school. The Rogers Locomotive Erecting Shop will be renovated using CETA and Local Public Works Act money to become an industrial museum and annex to the town library. One of the raceways is being made into a park and another mill building will become an arts and crafts center. A savings bank that has been a major force behind the recent adaption of warehouse and factory lofts to residential use in Manhattan announced in early 1978 that it would be the chief financier of a conversion of the Essex Mill into an apartment and commercial complex.

The hope is that people will be drawn into the narrow streets of the mill district and make them come alive again. The falls themselves are a powerful attraction; when the water is high dozens of cars can be seen in the lots of the park that now surrounds the falls. Brave visitors can venture out to points only a few feet from where the river drops eighty feet into the canyon below.

Downtown Paterson begins only a few blocks from the falls, and has great architectural potential, but is still economically shaky. A number of public and bank buildings are outstanding in design and detail. The City Hall shows the Beaux Arts style at its most exuberant. The neoclassic County Court House stands next to a very rare red and white brick Flemish Renaissance extravaganza that was once the Post Office but now serves as an annex to the Court House. All three buildings went up during the last decade of the nineteenth century, and all are in excellent condition. Commercial buildings downtown display sculptured lions and other ornaments, although many of these draw little attention from the tangle of signs and facade obliteration below.

Urban renewal has left its unfortunate mark on the commercial district. Too many blocks were demolished and cleared and too few planners' dreams materialized. Vast areas now serve only as parking lots, ostensibly to accommodate more shoppers, although the new shops and stores which were to attract them were supposed to go on the same sites. And that, in turn, was based on a new access road from the freeway that was never built. The whole thing sounds very confusing and has an appearance to match.

Meanwhile, just about every other stock answer to urban decline has been tried. A four lane loop road was to be built around downtown, but it wasn't finished, and the part that was has been supplied with cheap plastic light fixtures that have been badly vandalized. Huge high-rise public housing projects were built, but did little to ease the decay in surrounding neighborhoods. There are even the remnants of an embryonic effort to build a covered downtown mall; about half a block of the old market district was completed before the project was abandoned. Since then fire has gutted one of the buildings in the mall and some merchants have closed up their stores.

In short, little in the way of standard solutions seems to have had much positive effect on Paterson up to now. The rediscovery of the mill district and the successful initiation of a number of projects there holds a new kind of promise for the future—one built on Paterson's legacy as a gritty city. To some, it might appear a bit callous to focus the city's attention away from the traditional concerns of downtown revival and housing improvement. But clearly the direct approach has had limited results. That is what makes Paterson at once the most intriguing and the most disturbing city among the twelve; what the city has chosen to do is precisely the thesis of this book. It is seeking to build a viable economic base on the use, reuse, and adaptive use of the mills that once made it a great industrial city, and thereby to rejuvenate its commercial sector, provide housing opportunities, and spread the benefits of more employment to all its neighborhoods. Given the other options, it is worth a try, and it just might work.

2. *The Great Falls, 72 feet high, 280 feet wide, second to Niagara in the Eastern U.S.*

3. *Alexander Hamilton, founder of Paterson, in Great Falls Park*

4. *Factories below the falls*

5. *Protective gate above the falls with initials of the Society for Useful Manufactures*

6. *Tailrace of the Middle Raceway, 1792–1802*

7. *Detail of windows and lintels, Hamil Mill, Mill Street*

8. *Hamil Mill facade*

9. *Rogers Locomotive Company frame fitting shop and administration building, Spruce Street*

10. *Old burlesque theater, Van Houten Street, between the mills and downtown*

11. *Downtown office building,
Main and Market Streets*

12. *Shop near Police Headquarters
on Washington Street*

13. *Former Post Office (now Courthouse annex), Flemish Renaissance 1899; and Passaic County Courthouse, Neo-Renaissance 1903*

14. *City Hall*

15. *Dublin streetscape*

16. *Dublin overview*

READING

READING IS A MANUFACTURING CITY THAT WEARS ITS
image on its sleeve, from the carshops and yards of its famous
railroad up the hillsides to the last rowhouse nestled up against
the forest. The rowhouses, churches, and red brick warehouses
and factories are densely packed in a grid of streets that flaunts
its disrespect for the hilly terrain.

The grid was laid out in 1748 by surveyors reporting to
William Penn's son Thomas. The plan was to be a larger version
of the grid and central square used for Lancaster, with no particular concern for the fact that Lancaster is a flat city. Probably
the founders did not foresee that their successors would expand
the grid from the small level area around Penn Square up Mount
Penn to the east and into the steep-sided valley between Mount
Penn and Neversink Mountain.

Although there were a few Quakers keeping an eye on Reading's development in the interests of its founders, the city and
surrounding country were settled, like most of Eastern Pennsylvania, by a flood of German immigrants in the eighteenth and
early nineteenth centuries. The names on Reading's first list of
taxables were almost exclusively German. Although by 1890 all
but 8 percent of Reading's citizens were native-born Americans
the descendants of German immigrants clung to their traditions

Downtown across the Reading Railroad yards

and made the city seem far more foreign than it was. According to an 1881 Board of Trade appraisal of Reading, the inherited mixture of Teuton and Anglo-Saxon were responsible for the zeal and diligence with which the residents of Reading and surrounding Berks County developed their impressive manufacturing skills.

It all began with hats. In 1795 there were already thirty-eight hatters in Reading. By 1824 almost five hundred craftsmen were employed in the annual manufacture of 150,000 hats. These were sturdy sensible wool hats, all in black, with wide brims and tall crowns so stiff that they could bear the weight of a two-hundred-pound man. Colors were not added until 1847, and ladies' hats were not tried until 1878. By 1882 a total of twenty-five hat factories in Reading and Berks County shipped out over six million hats.

Hats were soon surpassed by iron and ironware. Berks County iron forges and furnaces went way back into the eighteenth century. The first blast furnace, built in 1824, was named after the great contemporary statesman Henry Clay. But the flowering of the iron industry in Reading came with the railroad which in 1842 tied Reading to the enormous anthracite beds thirty miles to the northwest, beyond Pottsville. In the following decade Reading attracted factories that made locomotive engines, nails, rifle barrels, steam engines, plows, and threshing machines. More factories were started to manufacture stoves, nuts and bolts, locks and chains so that by 1898 there were forty-eight establishments making iron and iron products.

The Philadelphia and Reading Railroad was responsible for this success. One of the first railroads in the country, it grew from ninety-four trunk miles in 1842 to over 840 miles of trunk and branches by 1881. At the turn of the century the railroad company had over five hundred locomotives and over twenty-two thousand cars and transported eight million tons of anthracite coal a year. The car yards were second only to Altoona's in importance in the nation. They employed three thousand workers and were such a stable source of Reading's wealth that in a contemporary appraisal Morton Montgomery concluded that "a great proportion of the substantial growth of Reading in buildings, stores, factories, churches and schools is directly attributable to the Company's disbursements." All this growth was not without its interruptions. For example, in 1839 the company suffered a strike of three hundred workers demanding an increase not only in wages but also in their whiskey quota, to one-and-a-half pints a day, to be doled out in nine equal doses. The management was relentless, the strike was to no avail, and work went on without the desired alcoholic reward.

The car yards are still used by Conrail at a modest level of activity, but the Reading railroad station is abandoned and the footbridges across the tracks have tumbled down. By 1930 Reading had shifted from heavy to light manufacturing. It became known for such products as hosiery, cigars and pretzels.

Built before zoning ordinances segregated uses, Reading's nineteenth-century factories were erected right in the middle of residential blocks. To contemporary eyes, the well-proportioned brickwork and ornamental facades add strength and variety to these residential streets. Yet, as in other cities, Reading's mill buildings became abandoned in the decades following World War II as they lost out to suburban locations.

Quite by accident, and with no assistance by city planners, Reading's entrepreneurs have invented an ingenious new use for the abandoned mill buildings—they have made Reading the Factory Outlet Capital of the East. The phenomenon is fondly described in a December 1977 *New Yorker* article by a writer who had used Reading as an eccentric weekend hideaway for years and suddenly discovered that hordes of tourist bargain-hunters were turning Reading into a far-from-eccentric place to shop.

As Calvin Trillin tells in his article, it all began in 1973 when the Reading-Berks County-Pennsylvania Dutch Travel Association suggested that some factory outlets join the association. A pamphlet, "Shopping Spree," was prepared and found to be in some demand. Then two different entrepreneurs acquired abandoned mill buildings in a crowded semi-residential area and turned them into two different city-block size factory outlet shopping centers with hundreds of different brand-name factory overruns and irregulars offered for sale on a percentage basis by their manufacturers.

The Great Factory Store and the Reading Outlet Center are several blocks apart on Moss Street near the Reading car yards. They are gaily decked with signs and banners and advertise energetically among women's groups in the surrounding states. An estimated four thousand tour busses visited Reading's outlet stores in 1977.

As the outlet boom has caught on, even local shoppers are being lured back from suburban malls. It has become fashionable to call oneself an outlet. Trillin found a refreshment stand on Moss Street calling itself "Ice Cream and Sandwich Outlet." Most important, the city fathers now see the far-reaching benefits of the outlets, and are encouraging their growth. What could be better than recycling old mill buildings and boosting retail sales and taxes at the same time?

In addition to being Pretzel Capital of the World, and now Factory Outlet Capital of the World, Reading could also lay claim to being the Valhalla of the Rowhouse. From the pagoda atop Mount Penn, Reading is a Harris tweed of rowhouses. There are two-story rowhouses and three-story rowhouses, plain rowhouses and rowhouses with porches, turrets or gables. In addition to workers' rowhouses, there are merchants' rowhouses and bankers' rowhouses in elegant clusters all over town. Almost all of them were built in the last half of the nineteenth century, when over fifteen thousand residences were built, 90 percent of them of brick.

Rowhouse construction was financed by a myriad of savings and loan societies, many of which were founded by groups of workers in the same factory. After 1876, the societies went beyond the mere financial role and entered directly into the construction of blocks of houses. Therefore, despite a wide variety of rowhouse styles, each block of houses in Reading is usually of a single style. Thus the repeating patterns that make the city so attractive today can be attributed in large part to the housing finance mechanism that grew up with the factories.

One early twentieth-century planner, John Nolen, much preferred detached garden district houses with fresh air and grass to the "unnecessary congestion" and "cheerlessness" of the "mass of unrelieved tin-roofed brick blocks with narrow straight streets." But what he described as this "unfortunate type of building so characteristic of the city" sold for $1,800 and rented for twelve dollars a month in 1910. Thanks to the rowhouse, Reading had one of the highest rates of homeownership and one of the lowest indices of crowding in the country.

Today, our eye has changed. The sight of an entire city of rowhouses on hills is a visual delight, especially rowhouses adorned like Reading's. In addition to the built-in ornaments of gables, turrets and porches, the rowhouses of Reading look like the world's largest display of awnings and Permastone. While neither of these features is on any architect's list of favorite details, where they appear in such profusion they force the discriminating eye to surrender to the overall effect.

Even more delightful are Reading's two aesthetic specialties—ironwork railings on curved porches and, most dazzling of all, stained glass windows of the most delicate design and colors. At least half of the rowhouses in Reading boast one or more beautiful stained glass windows. In many cases these lovely windows are somewhat incongruously framed in Permastone. One could spend days following the blocks around corners to find the most beautiful window of all.

And so we've come full circle. It has now been over a century since the savings and loan associations got into the business of housing construction and began putting up their rows. The intervening fashion for detached houses with ample yards seemed legitimate in its time. Now, however, the "unfortunate housing type"—the rowhouse—and the "unyielding" grid of streets seem good ways to save energy, reduce congestion and keep things at a human scale. The "hopeless" mix of housing and commercial uses is now looked to as a way of reducing crime and increasing urban vitality. As we build townhouses in the suburbs to recreate the sense of neighborhood that is missing there, a place like Reading becomes a source of ideas and even inspiration.

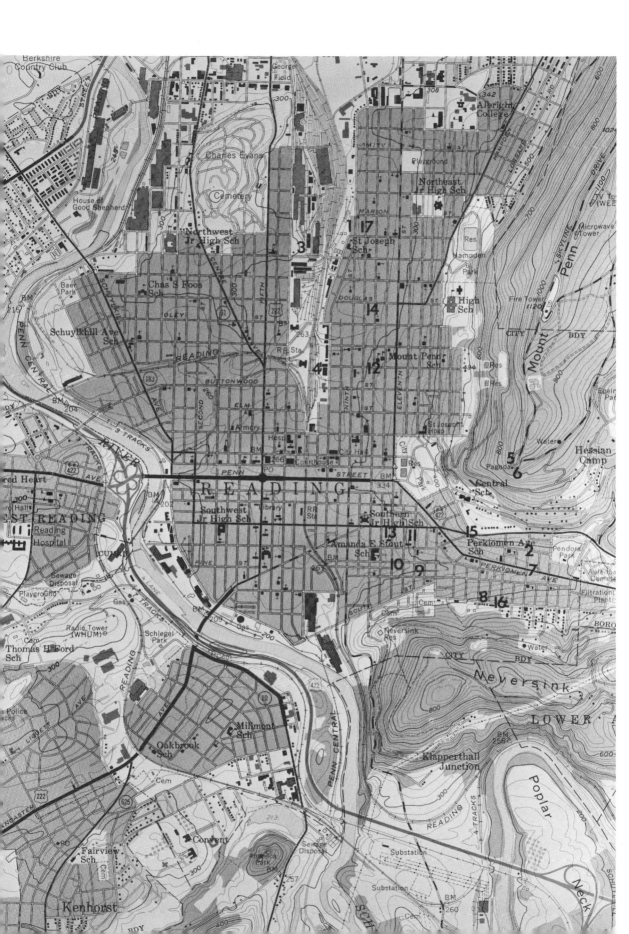

2. *Neighborhood off Perkiomen Avenue*

3. *Stockpiles at the railroad car shops*

4. Remains of a pedestrian bridge over the rail yards: abandoned passenger station on right

5. *Reading from the pagoda atop Mount Penn; car shops at top*

6. *Rowhouses from the pagoda*

7. *House on Perkiomen Avenue*

8. Backyards off Fairview Street

9. *Typical rowhouse curved porch and stained glass*

10. *Stained glass and permastone*

11. *Curved porch on Twelfth Street*

13. *Stained glass transom near Eleventh and Chestnut Streets*

12. *Barbershop on North Tenth Street*

14. *Rowhouses on North Tenth Street*

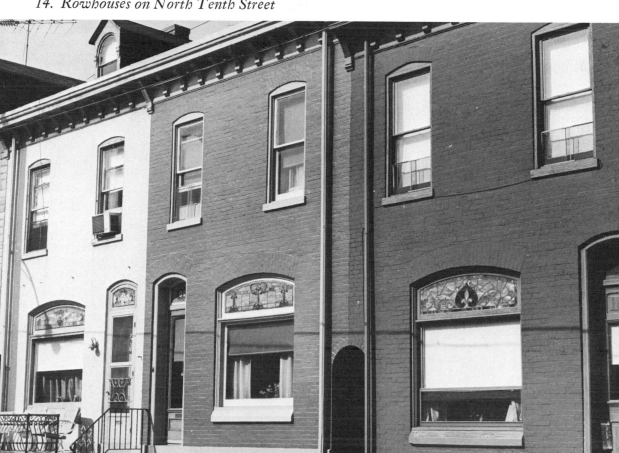

15. *Stone rowhouses on Clymer Street*

16. *View of the pagoda off Fairview Street*

17. *Factory outlet on Moss Street*

BUT FOR THE INTERVENTION OF A WELL-KNOWN LAND
speculator in the early years of the Republic, Air Force One
might today be home based in Trenton. In October of 1783,
Congress resolved to locate the national capital either on the
Delaware near Trenton, or on the Potomac near Georgetown.
George Washington, who with his friends had extensive land
holdings on the east side of the Potomac, argued successfully
that the unity of the Republic required the more southern location.

Trenton at that point was already well established, having
been founded in 1679 at "Ye ffalles of ye De La Warr." In what
must be one of history's first recorded comments on floodplain
management, the Indians dubbed the town Littleworth, thinking
it to be so close to the river that it would likely be washed away.
But in the three centuries since, Trenton has survived not only
floods, but three revolutions as well—the American, the Industrial, and the Bureaucratic.

Each of these has left its mark on the city. In contrast to other
gritty cities, which are attractive because of their consistency
and repetitive patterns, Trenton teases the eye with juxtaposi-
tions of different periods and different scales. When you turn

George Washington at Mill Hill, site of the Second Battle of Trenton, 1777

the corner in Trenton you cannot predict what will be there—
a restored colonial mansion, an old factory, a highrise state office
building, or maybe all three.

During the Revolutionary winter of 1776, Trenton was reluctant host to the brash Colonel Rall and his four thousand Hessian
troops; the town buzzed with conspiracies and everyone thought
everyone else to be a spy for the Continentals. On Christmas
night, the city established its patriotic reputation in the famous
rout of the Hessian soldiers following Washington's crossing of
the Delaware River. Washington followed that victory with a
second in January 1777.

Colonial buildings remain throughout downtown Trenton,
especially in the area around the Capitol. Particularly note-
worthy is the Old Barracks, the only remaining of five such
installations erected in New Jersey at the time of the French and
Indian War; it is now a museum. Nearby is the Mill Hill Historic District, named after the grist mill built by Mahlon Stacy,
Trenton's first settler in 1679. The site of Washington's second
battle with the Hessians is a largely residential section that has
already undergone extensive private renovation on Mercer and
Jackson Streets. Public investments have gone into new sidewalks, lighting, parks, and playgrounds, the latter two on the
site of the second battle itself. Efforts are now underway to
slowly and carefully expand the revitalization to nearby blocks
to the south and east.

A later era's legacy of the colonial era is the ornate Battle
Monument erected in 1891 at the site of Washington's first
Trenton victory. Today the monument is surrounded by a confusion of intersecting radials, old railroad yards, and tacky commercial and rundown residential buildings that in an odd way
make it more impressive than if it were set off forlornly in a
park somewhere.

The city is also trying to do something about this neighborhood. But in contrast to Mill Hill, where efforts are measured
and disruption is minimized, in the Monument area Trenton
seems to be staging a revival of all the mistakes and wrong-
headedness of classic urban renewal. Part of the problem is due

to the physical structure of the neighborhood; unlike self-contained Mill Hill, it spills out in all directions and meets few natural boundaries. Vacant lots already abound, and the residential densities appear quite low. But the other part of the problem is that the plans are far too bold to be achieved, and could well destroy what little community is left.

The Industrial Revolution came early to Trenton because its location gave it both water power and transportation advantages. In 1738 the first regular stage service from New Brunswick south to Trenton filled the need for an overland link between Philadelphia and New York City; passengers and freight would go by boat from Philadelphia to Trenton on the Delaware, take the stage to New Brunswick, and then travel down the Raritan and on to New York by boat. This gave Trenton importance as a stopover, since everyone had to wait for the freight to be shifted between land and water conveyances. By 1772 new coaches called "Flying Machines" cut the New York to Philadelphia trip to a day and a half, and made Trenton the most popular place to spend the night.

The opening of the Delaware and Raritan Canal through Trenton in 1834 provided the long-sought all water route between Philadelphia and New York. When the Canal opened, freight rates fell from $100 to $8 per ton between the two cities. The canal carried mostly freight (a parallel railroad carried passengers) and allowed Pennsylvania anthracite coal to reach New York from two sources: from the Pottsville coalfields via the Schuylkill Navigation and from the coalfields north of Allentown via the Lehigh Canal.

The Lehigh route made use of a feeder canal right through Trenton beginning in 1854. It is this improved feeder canal that today comprises what is left of this great canal system in Trenton; it snakes through the residential neighborhoods around and south of Cadwalader Park for several miles and ends up near the Battle Monument. The main canal coming up from Bordentown was long ago filled in by railroads and highways, but sections between Trenton and New Brunswick have been nicely restored as parks, an idea Trenton would like to bring into the city by building a linear park along the old feeder canal right of way.

In 1841, the Delaware and Raritan carried 120,000 tons of anthracite to New York City; by 1860 the volume had increased tenfold to over a million tons. This specialized bulk shipping kept the canals alive and contributing to the economy later in Trenton than in other cities, where railroads largely took over freight shipping. The availability of cheap coal also caused a great industrial complex to grow up where the routes came together at Trenton.

The three leading industries in Trenton during the nineteenth and early twentieth centuries were iron and steel, pottery and rubber. In all three cases Trenton took an early lead but lost it to other areas where raw materials and markets were more accessible.

The first iron works in Trenton dates from 1723; by 1750 the Benjamin Yard Steel Mill was one of the major facilities in the Colonies. The achievements of the local industry reached their peak, however, in the period 1847–67 when Trenton is credited with having produced the first wrought iron beams, and introduced the open hearth furnace to America. John A. Roebling was the first American to manufacture steel cable; the Brooklyn Bridge and the bridge over Niagara Falls are suspended from cables made in his mills in Trenton. The Roebling family shared their success by helping provide the city with a library, the city hall, and the hospital.

Like iron, pottery production in Trenton began in 1723, and the city still retains some of the oldest continuously operated potteries in America. Areas around Trenton contained clays that were very well suited to ceramic production. By 1880, the city was the leading pottery center in the country, with a product range that focused on china, hotelware, tile and bricks. The rows of plump kilns with their rounded and tapered chimneys were a landmark of Trenton for many years and gave an English look to the industrial areas.

In the latter years of the nineteenth century two individuals played important roles in the city's pottery industry. Walter

Scott Lenox, a native of Trenton who grew up around the kilns, achieved new American standards of quality for fine china. The other entrepreneur, Thomas Maddock, successfully developed the bathroom fixture industry in Trenton to the point where the city was called the "Staffordshire of America" after its English counterpart. From 1880–1910, 27 of the 47 euphemistically-named "sanitary-ware potteries" in America were in Trenton. In one year, 1895, all of the sanitary-ware produced in the U.S. came out of Trenton.

The decline of the pottery industry in Trenton had begun even before the turn of the century. A series of strikes in 1883 and 1884 resulted in many potteries either relocating or losing business to new factories in the Ohio Valley, where suitable clays had been discovered. Removal of the tariff on foreign pottery was proposed by President Cleveland in 1892 and caused an immediate depression as orders were cancelled in anticipation of the new competition. Many potteries were forced to combine to survive; Trenton Potteries emerged from a merger of five major firms. It was in turn purchased by Crane in 1922, when the industry was hit by a major lock-out strike in Trenton; the city never fully recovered its place in the industry.

The rubber industry lived an even more ephemeral existence in Trenton. There were some efforts at rubber production as early as 1850, but the heyday of the rubber industry in Trenton was the brief period between 1905 and 1920, when the city was the tire capital of the country. Auto tires at that time were of such poor quality that the geographical advantage lay with manufacturers close to population centers, since replacement tires were almost monthly purchases. But World War I brought demands for more durable products, and the technology was passed on to the consumer market. By 1920 the replacement tire industry in Trenton had pretty much collapsed and locations in Ohio, nearer to auto manufacturing centers, became preeminent.

While these three industries dominated the industrial period in Trenton, there have been other interesting specialties. Steam turbines and compressors have been a big business since 1901; but so has the production of children's dolls. Rocket fuel is another important product. And one Trenton company has been in the parachute business since 1920.

Many other industries have gone now, relocated in the suburbs or elsewhere. The headquarters for Roebling's steel works is now a county office building. The canals await efforts to restore them as parks and recreation areas. The working-class neighborhoods are still there, but the steel workers now commute to the Fairless Hills works in nearby Pennsylvania. Chambersburg, a predominently Italian neighborhood that backs up on the empty steel mills, is a particularly well-kept section of rows, duplexes, and single homes with manicured side yards. It still retains the corner stores, taverns and restaurants that have been there for decades.

Other neighborhoods have not survived as well. One of Trenton's problems is that the confusion of radial streets running in different directions has somehow resulted in poorly defined residential areas that are susceptible to blight. Projects like the restoration of the canal through Cadwalader Park and into downtown take on special importance in such cases because they can bring better structure and cohesiveness to their surroundings.

The shopping area of downtown Trenton is a victim of the same suburban competition felt in other gritty cities. The commercial decay is unfortunately not helped by the latest revival fad—construction of a pedestrian mall for three blocks along State Street. The result is to break the continuity of one of the most important streets in the city, a street that has historically brought various parts of the city together.

The loss of manufacturing and retailing jobs in Trenton has been matched by a gain in state employment. Around the Capitol along State Street the city looks prosperous and lively. But after work the parking lots around the glistening state office buildings empty out as everyone goes home to the suburbs. More high-rise state office buildings are planned or under construction, but they include their own parking and make it essentially unnecessary for state employees to spend much time at all outside the building. One hopeful sign is the recent conversion of an old furniture store on Broad Street into offices for the Division of Taxation. More thoughtful reuses and fewer self-contained towers would probably be a good recipe to revive downtown Trenton, but at this point the city seems willing to take whatever it can get in whatever form it comes from the state.

In a very real sense, Trenton today is an example of the post-industrial society. The major challenge the city faces is making those who work in Trenton want to live in Trenton. The resources to do that are there—in the canals that could become parks, the factories and warehouses that could be adapted to new commercial and other uses, and in the great variety of house types that are still in good condition. When you look at the experience of other gritty cities, you must conclude that Trenton is a city whose future lies in forgetting about bold solutions and redevelopment breakthroughs; the city frankly doesn't have the draw of money and people to make these work very well. Instead it needs to make better use of its potpourri of remnants and vestiges of all the things it has seen and been before.

2. *The Old Barracks, dating from the French and Indian War and used by both Hessians and Continentals*

3. The State Capitol and downtown Trenton from across the Delaware

4. *Old Masonic Temple (right) near the Capitol*

5. *The Trenton Battle Monument through the former Reading freight yard*

6. *The Delaware and Raritan Canal near State and Calhoun Streets*

7. *Detail, Van Sciver Building*

8. *Facade of the old Van Sciver furniture store converted to state offices, Broad Street*

9. Rear of the renovated Van Sciver Building

10. *North Broad Street near the Battle Monument*

11. *North Broad Street, Battle Monument in the distance*

12. Duplex near Cadwalader Park

13. Duplex in Chambersburg

14. *Rowhouses on Hanover Street near the Capitol*

15. *Colonial Avenue rowhouses off State Street*

16. *The State Museum on the Capitol grounds*

17. *South Clinton Avenue, Chambersburg, with the empty steel mills behind*

TROY

IF AN EDITION OF *THE NIGHT BEFORE CHRISTMAS* WERE
to be illustrated with scenes from the place it first appeared in
print, Saint Nicholas and his reindeer would skim over a long
thin city squeezed between the Hudson on the west and a line
of steep hills on the east. If you were to hunt down the original
Uncle Sam, you would find him overseeing the loading of pro-
visions for the Union Army on the Hudson River docks of the
same city. If Arrow Shirts were modeled for ads in the city of
their origin, young businessmen would be shown emerging
from elegant townhouse doorways with carved bay windows
overhead. All this was and much still is Troy, New York.

This odd-shaped city was an industrial powerhouse in the
mid-nineteenth century, second only to Pittsburgh in the production of iron and steel and seventeenth in population among
U.S. cities in 1840. Troy was the major city in the industrial
region that grew up below the falls of the Mohawk where that
river joined the Hudson. The region includes Cohoes, Green
Island, Watervliet and Waterford, each of which was a small
industrial city in its own right.

Evidence of Troy's remarkable early history can be found in
the ornate residential, commercial and public buildings of a
downtown that comes as close as any gritty city to real elegance.
Obvious wealth and a certain self-confidence created these
buildings.

Doorway on Third Street near Washington Park

Troy's growth slowed earlier than that of any other city in this book. By 1890 it had reached its present population of about sixty thousand and, although it climbed to a peak of seventy-six thousand in 1910, it had settled down into being a middle-sized city.

Beginning in the late nineteen-sixties, Troy's history of early industrialization began to be recognized as an asset. The Mohawk-Hudson area, including Troy, was selected as the site of the first major survey of structures significant in the development of American engineering. These studies expanded to make Troy one of the first beneficiaries of the fledgling discipline of industrial archeology.

The iron and steel industry flourished in Troy partly because of Troy's early transportation advantages tied to the rivers and canals. Troy was at the head of the tidal waters of the Hudson; the Erie Canal provided low-cost shipping from western coal beds, and the Champlain Canal linked up to Lake Champlain iron ore. Four railway lines linked Troy to other raw materials and to markets.

Troy, however, was also blessed with some remarkable inventor-entrepreneurs. The enormous Burden Iron Works resulted from a whole series of inventions by Henry Burden. His rotary concentric iron squeezer replaced the forge hammer in tempering iron. The horseshoe machine he patented in 1843 turned out 3,600 horseshoes per hour. At its peak, the Burden works produced fifty-one million shoes per year and made Troy the largest manufacturer of horseshoes in the world.

The equally enormous Albany and Rensselaer Iron and Steel Company resulted from a series of mergers of smaller companies. An owner of one of these, Alexander Lyman Holley, obtained the U.S. Bessemer Steel Process rights in 1863 and supervised the pioneer Bessemer plant in Troy in 1867. Two of these smaller companies set high standards for war production when they manufactured the rolled armor plate and rivets for the *Monitor*, which was launched only 101 days after the contract was signed.

Henry Ludlow began in 1866 to produce the valves he had invented, and his firm eventually became the largest in the nation. Several other valve companies established themselves in the

Troy industrial region, which also became a nationally important center of stove manufacture and bell casting.

Across the Hudson, in Cohoes, a massive textile complex grew up in the mid-nineteenth century around the falls of the Mohawk. About fifty textile mills used water power from the Mohawk River in the 1880's. The biggest complex, Harmony Mills, sprawls for two thousand feet along the cliffs below the falls. Four mansard-roofed towers frame a statue of one of the owners over the entrance of the famous Mastodon Mill (named for the prehistoric remains found during excavation for the building in 1866). Over three thousand workers were employed in the Harmony Mills in the 1880's; the company built over seven hundred neat brick dwelling units for its workers. Smaller plants in Cohoes such as the Ogden Mills also had handsome factory buildings and attractive worker housing.

A frustrated housewife, Hannah Montague, is said to have originated the idea that launched Troy into its textile specialty, detachable collars and cuffs. What started out as a small volume service for Mrs. Montague's fastidious husband and acquaintances ended up a business that employed over fifteen thousand people in 1925. Horace Greeley wrote that what he saw on a visit to the George Cluett collar and cuff factory around 1870, "would whiten a whole county with a linen snow storm of tens of thousands of flakes, in cuffs and wristlets, and collars and fronts and habits for ladies and gentlemen in every conceivable pattern at the rate of acres per day." Cluett-Peabody still maintains its corporate headquarters and the Arrow Shirt design division in Troy, as well as a one-room collar museum in testimony to the company's origins.

Although many of the earliest iron and steel complexes have long since succumbed to fire and collapse, attempts are underway in Troy to turn what remains of the area's industrial past into an indoor-outdoor museum of industrial history. The Hudson-Mohawk Industrial Gateway conducts weekend tours of mill structures, mill sites and canal remains. It published a walking tour in the local *Times Record* as part of a supplement on the region's industrial heritage. It is hoped to eventually tap some of the ten thousand tourists a day expected to visit Albany's Empire State Plaza, about twenty minutes' drive to the south.

The Gateway group was given the abandoned office building of the Burden Iron Company in south Troy which it hopes to use as its headquarters and for staging a sound and light show for tourists. Rebuilding the sixty-foot high Burden Company water wheel is an ambitious plan which would also attract people. The State of New York has been supportive of these efforts. A bill was enacted by the Legislature in 1977 creating the state's first urban cultural and industrial park in the Troy region, similar as has been done in Lowell, Massachusetts. The state has helped preserve the old Cluett-Peabody bleachery on Peebles Island by establishing there the restoration shops and conservation labs of the Recreation Department's Historic Preservation Division. It was in this bleachery that the sanforizing pre-shrinking process was developed in the late 1920's.

Concrete plans have not yet been made for aiding Troy's still-struggling downtown with this urban-industrial focus. A museum of industrial history could be located downtown in several fine old buildings to be vacated when their commercial occupants move into the downtown shopping mall soon to be completed. The fate is still uncertain of a whole strip of buildings along the river that were once the heart of the collar and cuff industry and are now half abandoned warehouses. Unlike almost all the other cities in this book, Troy is still demolishing parts of its downtown. Five of the River Street buildings were torn down in 1977, adding to the many blocks already vacant from demolition. Although the site is eligible for federal grants for restoration work, the remaining buildings could yet suffer a similar fate.

Thanks to some civic-minded citizens in the nineteenth century, Troy's downtown to the south of the urban renewal area is one of the most attractive that can be found. On one side of Third Street are a series of Gothic Revival buildings, formerly owned by the Emma Willard Female Seminary, and now part of Russell Sage College. Although the College has done its share of demolition, it has also preserved some old buildings along

Second Street for dormitories. Across Third Street is the delicately carved Hart Library and the Courthouse. Just north of these buildings is the Troy Savings Bank building, whose curving mansard roof shelters an acoustically fine music hall. Famous singers such as Jenny Lynd sang there in the nineteenth century. The hall is now used by the Philadelphia Orchestra as a recording studio when the orchestra is at its summer home at nearby Saratoga.

To the south of these fine public buildings, along Second, Third and Fifth Streets, Troy has quiet blocks of elegant rowhouse residences in brown, rust, olive, maroon, and an occasional beige. The most spectacular group surrounds Washington Park, a private enclosed park for the use of all owners and tenants of the buildings that face it. Several times a year the park hosts the public for fairs and festivals. Although many of the buildings were constructed in the first half of the nineteenth century, most of them acquired a feature in the late nineteenth century which is now a hallmark of Troy: a carved squared-off bay window. Dark stone and brick houses painted earth colors with these bay windows extend for blocks.

The proximity of tourists is not the only advantage Troy may derive from being just up the river from Albany. Troy shows signs of becoming a back-to-the-city bedroom community for state employees. Young middle-class couples and single people are buying old townhouses and fixing them up. Shameless bargains are turning into modest bargains, as prices rise. A neighborhood association encompassing several blocks from Washington Square north works with owners to obtain funds for renovation.

Troy's prospects are looking up. Many of the ingredients for revival as a city seem to be within reach, although some of the efforts are just beginning. The comeback of some neighborhoods, the lessons of past renewal efforts, and the attempts to rediscover the industrial past are all positive but very disparate undertakings scattered the length of the city. The question for Troy is whether it can figure out the right recipe and use these ingredients to serve up a success.

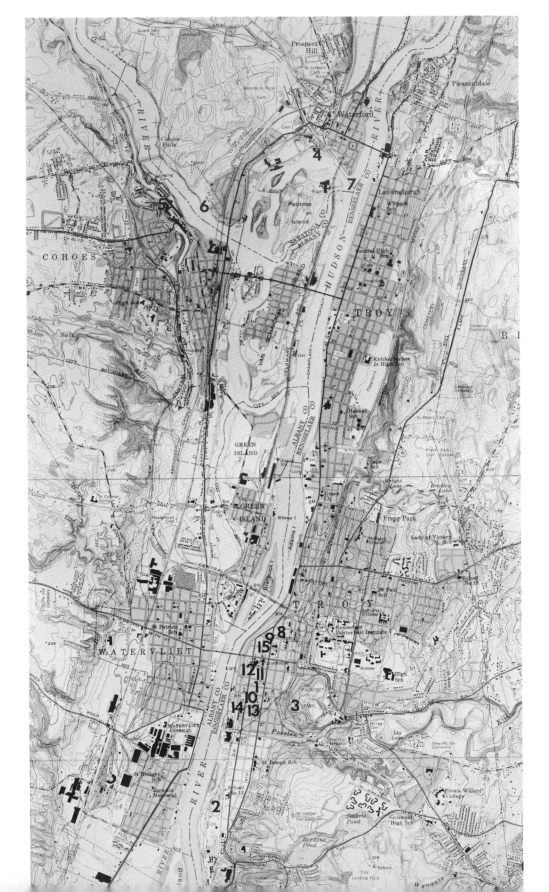

2. *Iron cauldron at the Burden Works ruins, 1903 Fortress Building in background*

3. Gasholder House (1873) from Prospect Park

4. *Laughlin Mill (1894) in Waterford, now owned by Ursula of Switzerland*

5. *Detail of Harmony Mill Number 3; note owner's statue in niche on facade*

6. *Harmony Mill Number 3 ("The Mastodon") in Cohoes (1868 and 1872)*

7. *Traffic sign at the confluence of the Hudson and the Mohawk, Waterford*

9. Urban renewal on Church Street downtown

10. Balcony on Washington Park

11. Detail, Hart Memorial Library on Third Street

13. Townhouses on Third Street

14. Townhouses and bay windows on Washington Park

WATERBURY

THE INDIANS CALLED IT MATTATUCK, FOR THE NATURAL
meadows bordering the Naugatuck River. The white settlers
incorporated the place in 1686 with the less flattering name of
Waterbury, for they recognized it as a swamp. In fact the soil
never was any good. It was despite this, or perhaps because of it,
that Waterbury came to national prominence as the center of
the U.S. brass industry. William Lathrop succinctly explains
why the brass industry got started at Waterbury, rather than
using the greater waterpower of the nearby Housatanic, or even
the better sites elsewhere on the Naugatuck: "Just here the soil
was poor. . . . Many left, some remained in poverty, a few laid
the foundations of the brass industry."

Thanks to Interstate 84, Waterbury's industrial nature is well
known to east-west travellers across Connecticut. The freeway
cuts through hills to the west and down into the Naugatuck
Valley and back up hills again to the east. Waterbury is dis-
played in all its grittiness: the red brick clock tower of the old
railroad station and the red brick of many old mills crowded
alongside the freeway. Although consolidating Waterbury's
image to outsiders, the freeway has exacerbated the physical
fragmentation of the city, which is also cut north-south by a
major highway. The downtown and most of the old mills are

1. Railroad station clock tower through the I-84/Conn. 8 interchange squeezed into the northeastern "quarter," while wooden residential neighborhoods fill the three other hilly "quarters." In spiritual counterpart to the complexity of its setting, Waterbury is still groping for a self-image in the late twentieth century that can do justice to its simple and powerful role in the late nineteenth.

In the early 1800's the odds were overwhelming that England would continue indefinitely as the major source of brass products in the newly formed United States. It was considered very difficult to overcome the English advantage in specialized machinery and, more important, in highly skilled workers.

Nonetheless, Alexander Hamilton urged a tariff on manufactured brassware in his Report on Manufactures. A tariff of 15 percent was levied in 1794; this was raised in steps over the nineteenth century to a peak of 45 percent in 1883. Behind the tariff's protection, a small group of manufacturers in Waterbury put together the business sense and technology to match the English.

The first brass was rolled for buttons from scrap copper kettles in 1802. That enterprise eventually became the Scovill Company, one of Waterbury's biggest. Another button company, eventually Benedict and Burnham, switched from ivory to brass buttons in 1823. The buttons were successfully sold throughout New England, thanks in part to the itinerant Connecticut peddlers who sold such items as buttons, cloth, clocks, and combs. English gilded buttons, however, were still much cheaper because the Americans did not yet understand the secrets of using only a few pennies worth of gold to gild.

There were some significant breakthroughs in the 1820's. After some unsuccessful attempts to hire skilled English craftsmen to teach them about brass making, the Scovill firm hired another Englishman, James Croft, who was able to pass on much technical information. In 1824 enormous brass rollers imported from England were installed at the Benedict button company. In 1831 another company, Holmes and Hotchkiss, was started with machinery from Birmingham, England. In 1836 they undertook the manufacture of hooks and eyes from wire and in 1842, straight pins. The crucial innovation in the making of pins was not in the manufacture of the pins themselves but the invention of a machine to stick them into a "paper of pins." Rights to the machine had to be acquired by the American Pin Company from all three inventors respectively of the three crucial parts: the "goose neck" which held the pins, the "slide" which spaced them, and the "crimper" which prepared the paper in folds to receive them.

Brass making in Waterbury got a further indirect boost in 1837 when Chauncy Jerome began the manufacture of a cheap brass clock in a nearby town, thereby assuring a steady demand. Waterbury began its own manufacture of clocks in 1857 with the Waterbury Clock Company. In 1880 the Waterbury Watch Company began the manufacture of watches, novelties at the time, which were made much fun of because they took so long to wind up. The marketing of a successful "quick winding" watch began in 1887. The Waterbury Clock Company came out with its own highly successful Ingersoll Dollar Watch around the turn of the century.

The manufacture of brasswares was a bootstrap operation throughout the nineteenth century. After the introduction of English skill and machinery, growth was stimulated from within Waterbury and the Naugatuck Valley itself. When Smith and Griggs started in the button and buckle business in 1865, for example, they sought help from the Scovill Company, where a number of their buckle dies were cut. Lathrop notes in his history of the brass industry that "except the first two firms, Scovill and Benedict before 1830, every other new undertaking in the Valley was inaugurated by men who gained experience in mills already existing." Copper was shipped from Michigan, zinc from Missouri and coal from Pennsylvania all the way to Connecticut because at the time the only labor skilled in the making and manufacture of brass was to be found in the Naugatuck Valley.

Manufacturers of pins, buckles and kettles got their rolled brass and wire locally—often from firms which shared directors with them. They got their machinery from local companies specializing in machinery for brassware. One, the Waterbury Farrel Foundry and Machine Company, advertised in the 1880's that it could produce machines for making any of the following: "spoons, lamps, bolts, nuts, locks, buttons, clocks, ferrules, jewelry, forks, burners, rivets, washers, hinges, buckles, watch cases, thimbles, steel springs, cartridges, etc."

Of such homely products was the wealth created that gave rise to the turn of the century boast that "Waterbury had something on everyone." And indeed Waterbury was responsible for the fittings on such essential items as the Wizard Cuff Holder, the Velvet Grip Loop and Haley's Magic Clasp, the Boston Garter and the Paris Garter. Warner Brothers corsets in Bridgeport depended on fine quality Smith and Griggs buttons from Waterbury. There was a bad time in 1880 when Warner Brothers returned 140 gross of buttons with the complaint that "these poor goods have nearly ruined [our] Hose Supporter trade."

Shoppers in present-day Waterbury are reminded of Waterbury's glorious past in their daily commercial dealings with such enterprises as Brass City Belt Company, Brass City Liquor Store, Brass City Paving Company, and Brass City Screw and Rivet Company. Waterbury's dominant role in the clock industry is far more dramatically symbolized by the 240 foot high tower on the former railroad station, now the headquarters of the *Waterbury Republican American* newspaper. Another handsome clock tower decorates the Green at the center of town and a third even smaller clock pillar stands in the sidewalk in Bank Street just off the Green.

Some of the brass and clock industry which made Waterbury well-known is still there. Scovill is still in Waterbury; it has diversified into the manufacture of household blenders and choppers under the name of Hamilton Beach. A second major brass company, the Chase, sold out to Kennecott Copper. The latter withdrew all manufacturing from Waterbury in the 1960's. A third major brass company, American Brass Company, was bought by Anaconda and has minor manufacturing in Waterbury. Some of the old mill buildings are still being used as part of these larger complexes, or are leased out to small companies. Many others were torn down to provide freeway rights-of-way.

One of the most visually spectacular efforts to convert a mill building for another use has transformed part of the old Ingersoll Dollar Watch factory on North Square into a Human Service Center, which houses a food coop, health clinic, food stamp offices, and other social welfare agencies. The project is being extended to another wing of the building to house more offices and a theater. It is hoped eventually to extend it still further to provide housing. This unusually successful effort was supported by an Economic Development Administration grant and organized by an entrepreneurial outgrowth of a former community action program agency called NOW (New Opportunities for Waterbury, Inc.).

The workers in the red brick mills by and large lived in wooden three decker detached apartment buildings, similar to working class housing in other New England industrial cities, but with a distinct Waterbury flavor. The characteristic Waterbury three deckers have three tiers of columned porches. Often the porches of the top two stories are half the width of the first floor porch and set off to one side. The backs of these buildings also have three tiers of porches, not rickety as a back porch might be expected to be, but solid and crisp with balustrades.

In the city's stable neighborhoods, such as the Italian-dominated Town Plot Hill and the Irish-dominated Hopeville, private care has kept the three deckers in good repair. A row of three deckers on the same block are usually painted in strikingly varied color combinations. Elsewhere in the city, in poorer and less stable neighborhoods, many three deckers have begun to deteriorate rapidly.

Government programs have had virtually no impact in countering problems of decay in Waterbury's neighborhoods. Only a small fraction of the funds made available to a rehabilitation loan program have been applied for by homeowners. In contrast to the city governments of Lancaster and Hoboken, the Waterbury planning and renewal officials gave little emphasis to housing rehabilitation, because it didn't seem worth bothering with a housing stock of wood.

Waterbury's downtown has an inviting focus. The Green, once a swamp, is a central commons covering two city blocks. It is a lovely park lined with benches and shaded by tall trees. To the south, off the Green, is a compact commercial district, parts of which have recently been spruced up with nice sidewalks and planters. Most of the buildings along these blocks have been built since 1902 when a devastating fire swept through downtown, destroying thirty-two buildings housing more than a hundred businesses.

These same blocks face a man-made threat today. Urban renewal officials, anxious to counter the decline in retail activity (caused in part by competition from the Naugatuck Valley Mall), are considering more demolition right off the Green and more high-rise construction. Most of downtown's character could be substantially disrupted; among other losses, both of Waterbury's unusually attractive family-run restaurants, Drescher's and Diorio's, are in blocks slated for demolition in the late 1970's.

Waterbury played as important a role in American industrial history as Troy or Paterson. Undoubtedly there is ample material in the old mill sites along the streams flowing into the Naugatuck to hold the interest of industrial archeologists and others for many years. But fire, highways and urban renewal have taken a stiff toll, countered by only sporadic efforts by Waterbury citizens to save the legacy of their past industrial glory. But by all rights, Waterbury ought to be in the same league as these other gritty cities that are finding their industrial roots and using them to grow on again. There's still a lot left; Waterbury must discover itself before it destroys itself.

2. *Benedict and Burnham brass mills on South Main Street*

3. *Scovill mills, Mill Street*

5. *Detail, Human Services Center*

6. *Human Services Center, North Square, former Waterbury Clock Co.*

7. *Renovated Odd Fellows Building on the Green*

8. Victorian neighborhood along Hillside Avenue

9. Commercial buildings along Grand Street

10. *The Waterbury Green*

11. Stained glass on West Main Street house

12. House on Fairview Street

13. Porch on Hillside Avenue

14. Detail, porch on Holmes Street

15. *House on Hillside Avenue*

16. Triple-deckers, Town Plot Hill

17. *Rear of a triple-decker on Town Plot Hill*

WILMINGTON

OF ALL THE GRITTY CITIES, WILMINGTON GOT OFF TO
the least auspicious start. The Swedes were the original settlers
in 1638. They built Fort Christina inland from the Delaware
River near the confluence of two smaller streams, one rushing
and one calm. Their homes were log cabins, the first seen in the
New World. But the Swedes had trouble attracting colonists
and supporting overseas colonies; in all, they sent twelve expe-
ditions to settle New Sweden, but by 1652 the number of colonists totalled only seventy-two. For their neighbors this was not
so bad, since the Swedes tended to get a little rough. At one
point, the Dutch found a gang from New Sweden merrily
tumbling houses and cutting down fruit trees at one of their
settlements near the mouth of the Schuylkill.

It is ironic that from such rude beginnings arose a city that
grew on its reputation for highly skilled industrial workers in
the nineteenth century, and became the nation's preeminent
center of corporate law in the twentieth. The origins of that
growth go back to the 1730's, when a group of Quaker businessmen from near Philadelphia noticed that the new farmlands being opened up to the west were drained by two river systems,
the Brandywine and the Christina, that converged on the Delaware at Wilmington. Both rivers offered routes to market for

Rodney Square, center of Wilmington's legal and corporate life

the grains and other products, and the Brandywine had the water power for mills to grind the grain. The town they built around the log cabins of the few remaining Swedes soon became the flour milling center of the colonies. Extensive shipping trade was also carried on; by 1789 Wilmington firms had eleven sloops and brigs in the West Indies trade alone.

As the eighteenth century came to a close, the city grew from a number of outside sources as well. Unrest in Ireland, insurrection in Santo Domingo, and revolution in France brought people of all economic levels, mainly because the ships they came on had Wilmington as home port. Louis Philippe spent part of his exile teaching math and language in Wilmington before returning to France to be crowned. One Frenchman who did not return was E. I. Du Pont, a student of Lavoisier and friend of Thomas Jefferson. At Jefferson's urging, Du Pont set up his powder mills on the Brandywine and began to produce an ever-increasing line of explosives for the expanding Republic. By the close of the War of 1812, Wilmington was a city of 4,400 people with a strong economy based on the mills on the Brandywine and the shipping on the Christina.

The 1840's were a decade of change for the city as the economy shifted from grain to industry. New railroads and canals in Pennsylvania allowed farmers to ship directly to the larger markets in Philadelphia, rather than down the rivers to Wilmington. Offsetting these losses of trade was the construction of several major railroad lines through the city. This gave Wilmington the dual advantages of big city transportation routes and rates and small city industrial land costs.

Meanwhile, the pace of life slowed on the Brandywine. Except for a few textile mills and Mr. Du Pont's black powder works, the river began a slow return to nature. Today it is graced by a series of parks and attractive bridges that begin in downtown Wilmington and go upstream for several miles to the grounds of the Hagley Museum, where the original Du Pont mills and storehouses are meticulously restored.

The major industries that grew up beside the railroad along the Christina were shipbuilding, railroad-car construction, carriage making, iron founding and tanning. All were locally owned, often by families active in the city's civic affairs; the head of a major car-wheel works was also the leader of the Masons and president of the Opera Society. The industries were also interrelated; for example, the leather was used to upholster the railroad cars, steamboats, and carriages. Much of this is documented in far greater detail in Carol Hoffecker's book on Wilmington between 1830 and 1910.

Over time the city gained a reputation for fine workmanship in its industries; Emperor Don Pedro of Brazil and King Oscar of Sweden were among those with private railroad cars made in Wilmington. Luxury steamships such as those used on the New York and Norwich Line were another specialty. By the end of the Civil War the four largest employers in Wilmington were in the railroad car and shipbuilding business. Two of them were among the four largest ironship builders in America in 1880.

Wilmington's pride in workmanship was based in some measure on the local ownership of the industries. Hoffecker points out that as the economy entered the period of trusts and cartels at the end of the nineteenth century, this advantage was lost as one by one the local plants were bought up and made part of much larger enterprises. In many cases the new owners viewed disdainfully the emphasis these factories had placed on quality in workmanship and luxury of detail. Money was to be made in volume and in the newer production facilities in the big cities of the east and midwest. In the course of a few years the plants along the Christina became little more than backup facilities to be used in times of great demand or labor troubles at other plants. Between 1899 and 1909, according to Hoffecker, Wilmington's industrial work force grew by only 1.1 percent while Trenton grew by 41.1 percent and Reading by 42.9. Except for some production of landing craft during World War II, the old factories along the Christina remain half-abandoned to this day, the weeds and trees slowly taking over in eerie contrast to the parks along the nearby Brandywine.

What saved Wilmington from decay was the decision by a group of aggressive young Du Pont cousins to build a downtown headquarters worthy of the world-wide reputation of the company they had recently inherited and were planning to expand into chemicals. The first section of the Du Pont Building on Rodney Square was completed in 1907. Two large additions, a hotel and a theater, were added soon after. In a few short years the economic base of the city shifted from industry to offices. To this day, the contrast of these can be seen in the impressive downtown towers and the old ethnic neighborhoods on the hillsides above the Christina and the railroad yards.

The early part of this century was also the era when the modern American corporation was developed. Delaware copied the liberal corporation chartering and operating laws of New Jersey, and when a reform-minded Governor named Woodrow Wilson saw to their repeal in New Jersey, Wilmington became the center of corporate law in the U.S. The subsequent frequency and range of opinions of Delaware courts on complex corporate management issues has established such a base of settled law (generally favorable to those in control) that Wilmington's preeminence is likely to go unchallenged for the forseeable future. This has brought an added air of prosperity and importance to the blocks surrounding the court houses on Rodney Square.

In recent years the face of Wilmington has been badly scarred by two man-made disasters—the urban renewal program and the construction of Interstate 95 through town. In the early years of the urban renewal program, Wilmington elected to use massive demolition and clearance in an effort to rid the city of what were thought to be slums. Wilmington was unique among the gritty cities in that its major ethnic group (until the arrival of Eastern Europeans and Italians around the turn of the century) was the blacks, who comprised about 10 percent of the population in the late nineteenth and early twentieth centuries. Most of the blacks lived in long-established neighborhoods east of downtown, where blocks of rowhouses, stores, and churches made up a virtually self-contained community.

Some of the churches were important in the development of black Protestant sects. The African Union Methodist Church, founded in 1812, was one of the first black corporations in the country and became the mother church to a conference of churches throughout the mid-Atlantic states. Hoffecker provides a vivid description of what that meant:

> *The African Methodist conference met four times each year. One of these quarterly meetings was traditionally held in Wilmington during August. This meeting, which was designated Big Quarterly, included the celebration of the founding of the conference. Big Quarterly, an event unique to Wilmington, was the principal holiday for black people from the Delmarva peninsula, southern Pennsylvania, and New Jersey. Thousands, both slave and free, descended on French Street wearing their finest apparel to attend services and meet with friends. Bands of spiritual singers and food vendors roamed the street. In pre-Civil War days, crowds estimated as large as 15,000 people participated in the event.*

The urban renewal program was quick and ruthless. Depending on how you count them in old photos and maps, about twenty-six blocks of the old black neighborhood were leveled, leaving a swath several blocks wide and most of the length of the city from the Christina to the Brandywine. Relocation efforts were minimal and the search for homes by the displaced in other neighborhoods destroyed the coherence and character of many other ethnic areas in the city, caused whites to flee, the housing market to tumble, and housing in some areas to be abandoned. A quarter of a century later, the city is just beginning to emerge from the chaos. The blocks that comprised the old black neighborhood are still vacant, except for the few predictable new public buildings that show blank walls and loading docks to the desolate acres.

The highway builders followed in the 1960's by running Interstate 95 right through the center of the city west of downtown. Once again neighborhoods were crippled, this time including many elegant turn of the century areas and one whole side of Cool Spring Park, once the most fashionable park in the city. In economic terms, the highway did little more than make it easier for people to move out to the suburbs and commute to the downtown office buildings. The continual "improvements" to the highway since it opened have meant almost constant further disruption to the surrounding areas; most recently a proposed connector to the railroad station has caused endless controversy and planner's blight over a large part of the city.

Given these events, it is a miracle the city survived at all. But the downtown business of corporations and law were unaffected by the disruptions and the office buildings kept rising. In an effort to revitalize downtown, Market Street was converted into a pedestrian mall from Rodney Square for six blocks south to 4th Street. The centerpiece of this impressive project is the restored Grand Opera House, a magnificent 1871 ironfront between 8th and 9th Streets.

Around the commercial area to the north and west are small areas where houses are being restored by private capital in what may be the beginnings of Wilmington's own back-to-the-city movement. Wilmington was never a fashion leader among cities, but in recent years its experience with abandonment and neighborhood instability have taught it some lessons. One of these has been passed on to dozens of other cities in the form of urban homesteading programs. Homesteading began in Wilmington when an aggressive young mayor decided to sell off for one dollar abandoned houses the city had taken title to, if the new owner agreed to bring the house up to standards and live in it. Condemned at first by urban experts as no solution to the housing problems of the poor, most of whom lacked the required capital and skills, the program slowly gained credibility as the public began to recognize the value homesteading provides for neighborhood stability and rejuvenation. The approach has been emulated by many other cities and was recently adopted as a significant part of federal housing programs. It is not dramatic, but it seems to be helping to save homes and neighborhoods.

And there is a great deal in Wilmington worth saving. There are still a number of well-preserved ethnic neighborhoods in the city. The portion of the East Side that survived the renewal program remains a physically isolated but viable black neighborhood. Old Swedes Church, part of it dating from 1698, serves as a center for the community. Little Italy and especially the commercial blocks along Union Street, and the Polish neighborhoods of Browntown and Hedgeville along Maryland Avenue comprise some of the most attractive and consistent ethnic areas in any of the gritty cities. Blocks of large and comfortable turn of the century homes are still to be seen along Franklin and Broom Streets and Delaware Avenue. West of Union Street are a number of residential areas, some built by the Bancrofts and the Du Ponts, in the Ebenezer Howard "Garden City" motif. And the city park system remains remarkable for its extent, variety, and beauty.

History has not treated Wilmington well. The wrenching shifts every few decades in its economic base, and the physical and social disruption of urban renewal and highway construction have left their mark on the city. It almost seems that no sooner has it recovered from one calamity before another overtakes it. Yet it somehow seems able to pick itself up, dust itself off, and keep on trying. When all is said and done, that small band of tough Swedes many well have had an influence after all.

2. Walker's Mill on the Brandywine above Rising Sun Lane

3. Wilson Liner at the old shipyards on the Christina

4. Bridges in Brandywine Park

5. Headquarters for one of the old shipbuilding firms on the Christina

6. *Adams Street and downtown from across the I-95 canyon*

7. *Old City Hall, Market Street Mall*

9. *Downtown and St. Hedwig's Church from Kosciusko Park*

10. *Rowhouses in Hedgeville, off Maryland Avenue*

11. *Duplexes near Baynard Boulevard*

12. Oak Street above Maryland Avenue

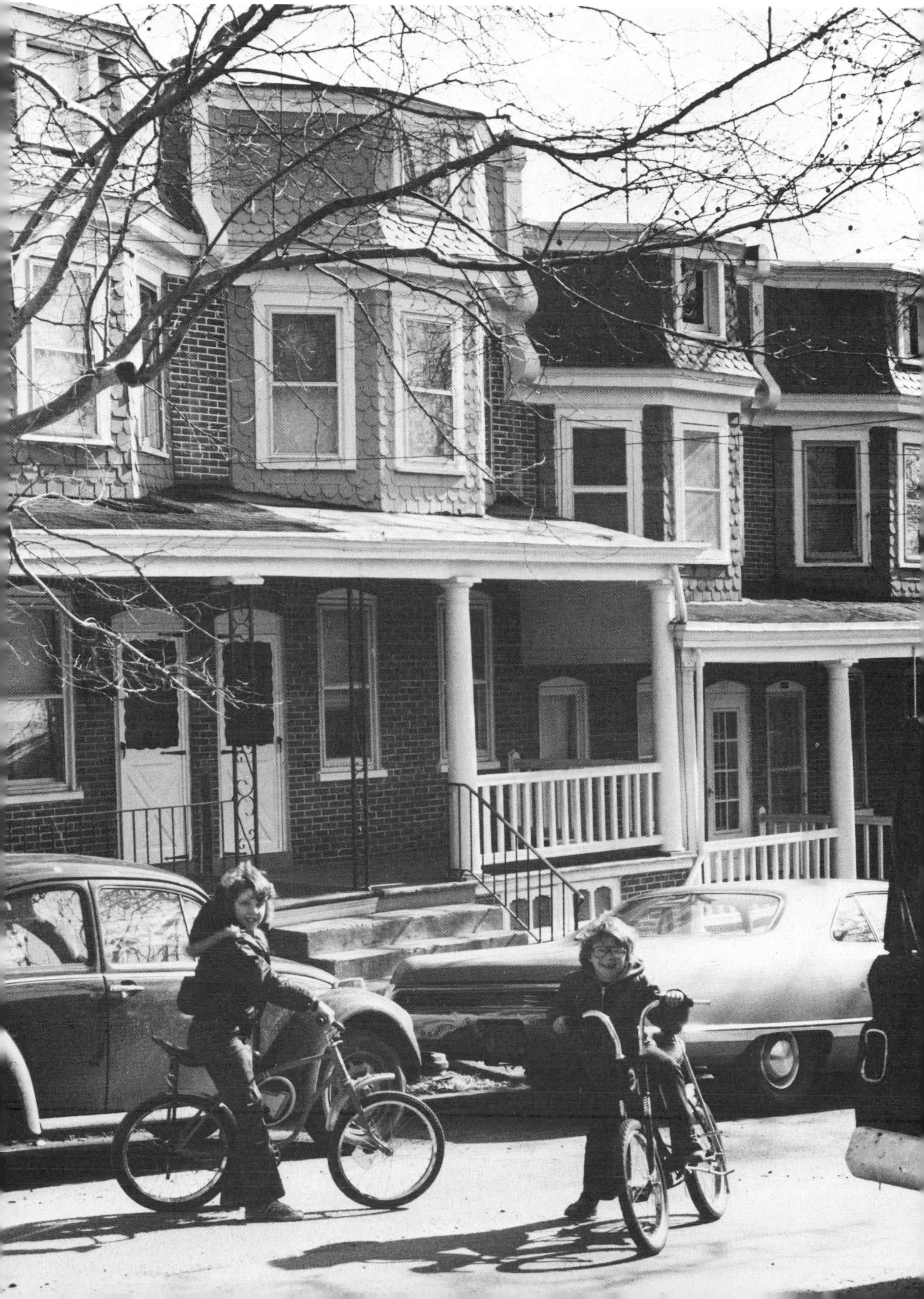

13. Johnny's Market, Maryland Avenue in Browntown

14. Sub shop in Little Italy, Lincoln Street

15. Franklin Street below Sixth Street

16. Houses on Fourteenth Street near Tatnall Street

SOURCES

The sources used in preparing the text are described below, beginning with general sources and continuing with a section of sources on each city. Following this list of sources there is a short list of books and articles that are suggested for further reading on the role of the gritty cities in the industrial revolution.

General

Our two basic sources for the introductory section on the gritty cities in the industrial revolution were *The Spatial Dynamics of U.S. Urban-Industrial Growth 1800–1914: Interpretive and Theoretical Essays* by Allan R. Pred (Cambridge, Mass.: Massachusetts Institute of Technology Press, 1966) and *Prisoners of Progress: American Industrial Cities 1850–1920* by Maury Klein and Harvey Kantor (New York: Macmillan & Co., 1976). Both books have useful statistical analyses of many aspects of the relationship between industrial and urban growth. The Pred book supplied in addition a clear framework for analysis of why some cities remained middle-sized.

We also obtained valuable information on canals, especially the Lehigh (for Allentown), the Delaware and Raritan and connecting canals (for Trenton), and the Erie Canal (for Troy) from *Canal Days in America: The History and Romance of Old Towpaths and Waterways* by Harry Sinclair Drago (New

York: Bramhall House, 1972). Some colorful quotes on particular industries came from *The Great Industries of the United States* by Horace Greeley (2 vols.; Hartford, Conn.: J. B. Burr, Hyde & Co., 1872). *The Report on the Social Statistics of Cities*, compiled by George E. Waring, Jr. (2 vols.; Washington, D.C. 1886; reprinted New York: Arno Press 1970) compiles statistics city-by-city on such amenities as parks and beer gardens.

Allentown

Sources on Allentown are skimpy and dominated by Chamber of Commerce publications. Relevant information is also available on the Lehigh Canal (from *Canal Days in America*, cited above), the cement industry and the origins of Mack trucks.

The Chamber of Commerce publications include a book of photos and brief captions of factories, downtown, and lavish residences (*Allentown, Pa.*, 1908), a tiny pamphlet (*The Clean City Invites You*, 1921) and a recent boosting booklet (*Allentown-Lehigh County, Pennsylvania*, 1974) that has considerable information on such amenities as Allentown's parks, bands and downtown retail center.

Our source on the cement industry was a booklet based on a conference paper by Samuel Joseph Young, *The Cement Industry: Its Origin and Growth* (Princeton, N.J.: Princeton University Press, 1939). Two books provided information on the origins of Mack trucks: *Trucks and Vans: 1892–1927* by Prince J. Marshall and Denis Bishop (New York: Macmillan, 1972) and *A History of Commercial Vehicles of the World* by J. F. Kuipers (Lingfield: Oakwood Press, 1972).

Two large booklets provided information on Allentown's early history: *A History of Trout Hall* by Charles Roberts (Allentown, Pa.: 1948) describes events associated with the Allen family mansion, and *Historic Allentown*, published by the Trexler Funeral Home in Allentown (1941), is readable and informative despite its surprising origins.

Bethlehem

Sources on Bethlehem are dominated by two magnificently illustrated excellent books written by the Bethlehem Book Committee and published by the Bethlehem Chamber of Commerce: *Bethlehem of Pennsylvania: The First One Hundred Years* (Bethlehem, 1968), and *Bethlehem of Pennsylvania; The Golden Years 1841–1920.* (Bethlehem, 1976). These books cover social and religious history, as well as political and industrial history, in a manner matched by few other sources on any of the twelve cities. The section on Bethlehem draws heavily on material from these two books.

Information on contemporary Bethlehem is available from a visitors' pamphlet, *Historic Bethlehem: The Walking and Riding Tours,* and a Chamber of Commerce publication, *Bethlehem: Quality of Life.*

Bridgeport

The two chief sources for Bridgeport were *Bridgeport and Vicinity*, edited by George Waldo, Jr. (2 vols., New York: S. J. Clarke, 1917) and *Story of Bridgeport 1836–1936* by Elsie Nicholas Danenberg (Bridgeport: Bridgeport Centennial Inc., 1936). The first volume of the Waldo book is narrative history with good chapters on transportation and industry; the second has biographies, including a long sketch on P. T. Barnum. The Danenberg book is a large, illustrated and readable history, prepared for the city's centennial. Interesting information on industry and physical layout is also to be found in two versions of John Nolen's planning study for Bridgeport: *Preliminary Report to the City Plan Commission* (1915) and *Better City Planning for Bridgeport* (1916), both published in Bridgeport.

Hoboken

The section on Hoboken is based in large part on a set of essays prepared for an American studies program at Stevens Institute: *Hoboken: A Collection of Essays* edited by Edward Halsey Foster and Geoffrey W. Clark (New York: Irving Publishers, Inc., 1976). We used material from essays covering Hoboken's history, politics and contribution to film history through *On The Waterfront.*

We also used more recent materials: *Hoboken 1976* is a bicentennial calendar with a historical introduction, published by the Hoboken City Government; The City of Hoboken's *Neighborhood Preservation Program*, a leaflet supplying basic information on the city's housing rehabilitation programs; *Hoboken . . . Reaching Out to Tomorrow* (1975) is a large booklet on Hoboken's community development program, and "Ho-Ho-Ho Hoboken Has the Last Laugh" (*Washington Post*, Nov. 10, 1976, p. A1).

Lancaster

The most useful early source on Lancaster is *Resources and Industries of the City of Lancaster* by W. Hensel (Lancaster: for the Lancaster Board of Trade, 1887). This book has good information on industry in Lancaster and a clear map of industrial locations in 1887. A source of information on Thaddeus Stevens and James Buchanan is *Lancaster's Golden Century 1821–1921: A Chronicle of Men and Women who Planned and Toiled to Build a City Strong and Beautiful* by H. M. J. Klein (Lancaster: Hager and Bro., 1921).

Contemporary materials on Lancaster include a booklet with miscellaneous history served up with walking tours, *Historic Heart of Lancaster: A Do-It-Yourself Guide For a Walking Tour of the Central Section of Lancaster, Pennsylvania, America's Oldest Inland City and County Seat of the Garden Spot of the World* by Gerald Lestz (Lancaster: John Baer's Sons, 1962). Another large booklet, *Lancaster, Pennsylvania*, published by the Chamber of Commerce in 1972, gives basic information on current industries and tourism. *The Annual Report for Lancaster, Pa. 1977–78* is an informative illustrated report on the city's redevelopment and community services programs. Finally, there are two impressive design guides: *Lancaster's Architecture: the Past's Gift to the City's Future* (catalogue of an exhibit organized by the Junior League, 1976) and *Lancaster, Pennsylvania: A Design Guide* (1977), a beautifully laid-out booklet prepared for the Lancaster city government for distribution to downtown merchants.

Norwich

The sources for Norwich include three late nineteenth-century histories which collectively provide rather skimpy information. *The History of Norwich to 1873* by Frances M. Caulkins (New London, Conn.: published privately, 1874) is loosely anecdotal.

The Leading Businessmen of Norwich by William H. Beckford (Boston: Mercantile Publishing Co. 1890) covers subjects in Norwich history well beyond the limited focus of its title. Finally *Norwich: The Rose of New England* by Leonard W. Bacon (Norwich: Cranston & Co. 1896) is a small but entertaining illustrated description of life in Norwich near the turn of the century.

Far richer, although more specialized, information is available on Norwich's role as the crucial link between steamboat and rail on the route between New York and Boston in the mid-nineteenth-century, in *The Quickest Route: The History of the Norwich and Worcester Railroad* by Elmer F. Farnham (Chester, Conn.: Pequot Press, 1973).

Paterson

Much of the information on Paterson comes from a fine collection of essays produced for a symposium on industrial archeology held in Paterson in 1974. They were published in the journal of the Council for Northeast Historical Archeology, *Northeast Historical Archeology*, Spring 1975. From this source we drew our material on the emigration of the English silk workers, the innovations of Rogers in the locomotive industry and information on mill architecture.

In addition we obtained material on the silk strike from Patrick Renshaw, *The Wobblies* (Garden City, N.Y.: Doubleday & Co., 1967), and biographical information on Jacob Rogers from *Random Collections* by Charles A. Shriner (Paterson: private printing, 1941). We obtained much useful information on Paterson's industrial development from *History of Industrial Paterson* by Levi R. Trumbull (Paterson: C. M. Herrick, printer, 1882).

The Paterson Department of Community Development provided material on the formation of the Great Falls Historic District and on the history of Paterson's downtown buildings.

Reading

The basic histories of Reading used for our text include: the *Annual Report* (1881) of the Reading Board of Trade, a remarkably detailed industrial history; *History of Reading and*

Proceedings of Sesquicentennial by Morton Montgomery (Reading: Times Book print, 1898); and *Two Centuries of Reading 1748–1948* by Raymond Albright (Reading: Historical Society of Berks County, 1948).

More specialized information on the early physical plan for Reading came from *The Foundation of the Town of Reading* by J. Bennett Nolan (Reading, 1929), and on a garden city planner's attitude towards a city like Reading from John Nolen's *Replanning Reading, an Industrial City of 100,000* (Boston: G. H. Ellis Co., 1910). An article in the *New Yorker* (Dec. 5, 1977), "U.S. Journal: Reading, Pa." by Calvin Trillin was our source of information on the boom in factory outlet stores in Reading.

Trenton

The best source of information on Trenton's industrial development is *The Trenton Story* by Eleanore Nolan Shulman (Trenton: MacCrellish & Quigley Co., 1958). Our chief source for the early history of Trenton is *History of Trenton 1679–1929* (published for the Trenton Historical Society, Princeton, N.J.: Princeton University Press, 1929). We used information from two other histories: *History of Trenton, N.J.* by Francis Lee (Trenton: J. L. Murphy, printer, 1895) and *The Greater Trenton N.J. Story* (published for the Chamber of Commerce, Trenton: Windsor Publications, 1967).

Trenton Old and New by Harry J. Podmore (Trenton: printed by MacCrellish & Quigley Co., 1964) describes historical buildings, many of which have long since disappeared. We also drew on materials prepared for the Department of City Planning for information about current restoration and urban renewal projects.

Troy

For Troy's industrial history, we relied heavily on *A Report of the Mohawk-Hudson Area Survey*, edited by Robert M. Vogel (Washington, D.C.; Smithsonian Institution Press, 1973). This is a collection of essays resulting from a 1969 survey conducted by a team of industrial archeologists organized by the Historic

American Engineering Record. *The City of Troy and its Vicinity* by Arthur J. Weise (Troy: Edward Green, 1886) is another rich source of information, especially on the industrial history of Troy and contiguous cities, arranged rather mysteriously in alphabetical order. Useful biographical information is available from Samuel Reznick's *Profiles out of the Past of Troy New York since 1789* (Troy: 1970). Rutherford Haynoy's *Troy and Rensselaer County, New York: A History* (1925) has cultural as well as governmental and business history.

Waterbury

Our basic information on the brass industry came from *The Brass Industry in Connecticut: A Study of the Origin and Development of the Brass Industry in the Naugatuck Valley* by William Lathrop (Shelton, Conn.: W. G. Lathrop, 1909). Some additional detail came from the interesting case study *Small Business in Brass Manufacturing: The Smith and Griggs Manufacturing Company of Waterbury* by Theodore F. Marburg (New York: New York University Press, 1956).

We also used material from two well-organized basic histories: *The Town and City of Waterbury from the Aboriginal Period to the Year 1895* by Joseph Anderson (3 vols; New Haven: Price & Lee Co., 1896), and *History of Waterbury and the Naugatuck Valley* by William Pape (New York: S. J. Clarke, 1918). *Waterbury and Her Industries* by Homer Bassett (Gardner, Mass., 1889) contains photographs and explanatory information on industries. Finally, a recent book, *Waterbury 1674 to 1974: A Pictorial History* by the Mattatuck Historical Society (Chester, Conn.: Pequot Press, 1974) has over two hundred photographs of Waterbury's past as well as some capsule history.

Wilmington

The section of Wilmington is substantially based on information found in *Wilmington, Delaware: Portrait of an Industrial City 1830–1910* by Carol E. Hoffecker (Published by the University Press of Virginia for the Eleutherian Mills-Hagley Foundation, 1974). The book has material on Wilmington's industrial history and physical development as well as some insights into the process of urbanization which were valuable in understanding other gritty cities. *Wilmington Delaware: Its Productive Industries and Commercial and Maritime Advantages* by A. J. Clement (Wilmington, Del.: published by the Board of Trade, 1888) contains unrestrained exuberant descriptions of every last one of Wilmington's industries. *Wilmington, Delaware: Three Centuries Under Four Flags* by Anna T. Lincoln (First published 1937; reprinted Port Washington, N.Y.: Kennikat Press, 1972) was our source on Wilmington's early history.

Selected Readings

Albion, Robert G. *The Rise of New York Port: 1815–1860.* New York: Charles Scribner's Sons, 1939.

Barton, Josef. *Peasants and Strangers: Italians, Rumanians, and Slovaks in an American City, 1890–1950.* Harvard Studies in Urban History. Cambridge, Mass.: Harvard University Press, 1975.

Blumin, Stuart. *The Urban Threshold: Growth and Change in a Nineteenth-Century American Community.* Chicago: The University of Chicago Press, 1976.

Borchert, John R. "American Metropolitan Evolution." *The Geographical Review*, Vol. 57, No. 3 (July, 1967), pp. 301–332.

Dawley, Alan. *Class and Community: The Industrial Revolution in Lynn.* Harvard Studies in Urban History. Cambridge, Mass.: Harvard University Press, 1976.

Duncan, Beverly and Stanley Lieberson. *Metropolis and Region in Transition.* Beverly Hills, Calif.: Sage Publications, 1970.

Elazar, Daniel J. *Cities of the Prairie: The Metropolitan Frontier and American Politics.* New York: Basic Books, 1970.

Frisch, Michael. *Town into City: Springfield, Massachusetts and the Meaning of Community, 1840–1880.* Harvard Studies in Urban History. Cambridge, Mass.: Harvard University Press, 1972.

Gitelman, Howard M. *Workingmen of Waltham: Mobility in American Urban Industrial Development, 1850–1890*. Baltimore: The Johns Hopkins University Press, 1974.

Goheen, Peter. "Industrialization and the Growth of Cities in Nineteenth-Century America." *American Studies*, Vol. XIV, No. 1 (Spring, 1973), pp. 49–65.

Griffen, Clyde and Sally Griffen. *Natives and Newcomers: The Ordering of Opportunity in Mid-Nineteenth-Century Poughkeepsie*. Harvard Studies in Urban History. Cambridge, Mass.: Harvard University Press, 1978.

Gutman, Herbert G. *Work, Culture, and Society in Industrializing America: Essays in American Working-Class and Social History*. New York: Alfred A. Knopf, 1976.

Kirkland, Edward C. *Men, Cities, and Transportation; A Study in New England History, 1820–1900*. Cambridge, Mass.: Harvard University Press.

Livingood, James W. *The Philadelphia-Baltimore Trade Rivalry, 1780–1860*. Harrisburg, Pa.: Pennsylvania Historical Commission, 1947.

McKelvey, Blake. *The Urbanization of America, 1860–1915*. New Brunswick, N.J.: Rutgers University Press, 1963.

McKenzie, Roderick D. *The Metropolitan Community*. New York: McGraw-Hill Book Co., 1933.

Moses, Leon and Harold F. Williamson, Jr. "The Location of Economic Activity in Cities." *The American Economic Review*, Vol. LVIII, No. 2 (May, 1967), pp. 211–222.

Pred, Allan. *Urban Growth and the Circulation of Information: The United States System of Cities, 1770–1840*. Harvard Studies in Urban History. Cambridge, Mass.: Harvard University Press, 1973.

Taylor, George Rodgers. *The Transportation Revolution, 1815–1860*. New York: Holt, Rinehart and Winston, 1951.

Thernstrom, Stephan. *Poverty and Progress: Social Mobility in a Nineteenth Century City*. Cambridge, Mass.: Harvard University Press, 1964.

Thernstrom, Stephan and Richard Sennett, eds. *Nineteenth-Century Cities: Essays in the New Urban History*. New Haven, Ct.: Yale University Press, 1969.

Ward, David. *Cities and Immigrants: A Geography of Change in Nineteenth Century America*. Historical Geography of North America Series. New York: Oxford University Press, 1971.

Warner, Sam Bass, Jr. *Streetcar Suburbs: The Process of Growth in Boston, 1870–1900*. Cambridge, Mass.: Harvard University Press, 1962.

Weber, Adna F. *The Growth of Cities in the Nineteenth Century; A Study in Statistics*. Cornell Reprints in Urban Studies. Ithaca, N.Y.: Cornell University Press, 1963.